SET YOURSELF ON FIRE!

HOW TO IGNITE YOUR PASSIONS AND LIVE THE LIFE YOU LOVE!

Phil Taylor

SET YOURSELF ON FIRE!

HOW TO IGNITE YOUR PASSIONS AND LIVE THE LIFE YOU LOVE!

Phil Taylor

TREMENDOUS
LIFE BOOKS.com

Set Yourself on Fire!

Published by
Tremendous Life Books
206 West Allen Street
Mechanicsburg, PA 17055

Copyright © 2010 by Phil Taylor

ISBN: 978-1-933715-93-3

Printed in the United States of America

DEDICATED TO

My loving mother, for whom words can never adequately express the deep appreciation for her profound love, faith, and constant prayers, which have sustained, encouraged, and fanned the flickering flame that burned within me. If there was anyone who demonstrated a life of fullness—the essence of the message of this book—and one whose life is truly set on fire!—ablaze with love, passion, goodness, kindness, enthusiasm, strength, joy, and hope—it is my dearest and most precious mom!

With a heart of unspeakable appreciation to you and for you, God bless you, Mom!

Your son,
Philip

"Strength and dignity are her clothing, and she smiles at the future. She opens her mouth in wisdom, and the teaching of kindness is on her tongue. Her children rise up and bless her."—Proverbs 31:25, 26, 28

Marguerite Giguère Taylor

"When you set yourself on fire, people love to come and see you burn."

John Wesley
Evangelist, Founder of Methodism 1703–1791

CONTENTS

ACKNOWLEDGMENTS

A heart of profound gratitude goes out to the wonderful team of individuals who made this book possible!

There is no doubt that as with everything else in life, it takes a team to make a project of this magnitude a true success! There is an endless list of people to thank, and it would fill the pages of this book to mention them all. Having said that, I would like to extend my very special thanks to the magnificent contribution of the following individuals.

Dilip Abayasekara, who initially read the manuscript, lit the match, put things in motion, and gave me the faith and encouragement to pursue this message with you!

Tracey Jones, for your enormous encouragement and for providing the extraordinary opportunity for this book to be published—you are Tremendous!

Jason Liller, for your solid support and guidance. You are a class act. Thank you!

Patrice Stephens-Bourgeault, for your unbelievable love, encouragement, and assistance in the first round of editing for this book. Thank you for your never-ceasing faith—you are on fire!

Laurent Bourgeault, a true statesman, for your thorough research and tireless effort in ensuring the accuracy of the information imparted in this book.

Bob Land, for your professional expertise and diligence in perfecting the editing process with such precision and care.

Benjamin Bachman, for the outstanding creative design of our cover—capturing the essence of *Set Yourself on Fire* with such wonderful imagery and artistry!

Gregory Dixon, for your extraordinary leadership with the management and coordination of the production process, thus ensuring that all the pieces of this project fit in perfectly. Greg, you personify the meaning of the message declaring that it takes a team to win! Thank you from the bottom of my heart!

For the members of my personal GoalAchievers group—Clark, Elena, Eva, Kyle, Maila, Martin, Mike, Nellie, Simon, and Soojin—who provided the weekly insight, guidance, and encouragement to keep on keeping on! This book belongs to each one of you!

To my loving mom, without whom this book would never be possible—had she not encouraged and believed in me, as she has throughout my entire life!

To Iwanda, my dearest and closest friend, the one who constantly evokes a warmth in my heart and a smile on my face, and who has lovingly supported and encouraged me through it all! Here's to Sweet Home Alabama!

Most of all, to God—the source of my joy, strength, and enthusiasm, and the One who has imparted an understanding and experience of all that is praiseworthy, loving, and good. How can words possibly and adequately express all that you are and all that you have given me? You are my first Love, to whom and for whom I owe my entire life!

And finally to each one of you! Thank you for investing in this book and being partners in this empowering message of hope! May you be encouraged and enormously blessed!

With a heart filled with gratitude,
Phil Taylor

FOREWORD

Parker J. Palmer wrote, "Each of us is a master at something, and part of becoming fully alive is to discover and develop our birthright competence." This wonderfully inspiring book by Phil Taylor is chock-full of inspiration and ideas for any person who wants to become fully alive—in other words, *Set Yourself on Fire!*

I believe that one reason that Phil Taylor's book is packed with dynamic energy and illuminating insights is because it is a reflection of the author. If you hear Phil speak, his sheer enthusiasm, love of life, and genuinely caring nature will leap out at you. He writes with the power of authenticity and life experience. The message of this book warms my heart, quickens my spirit, and challenges me to live up to my dreams.

My own experience in searching for and claiming the life and vocation that the master designer of the universe intended for me validates the truths espoused in this book. It matters not what your occupation is, how much you are earning, and how much stuff you have; what matters is, whether you are living a life that is consistent with your natural gifts, that conforms to the highest values of your heart, and the calling of the voice of Divinity within you.

If you, the reader, find that your life is not where you want it to be, I invite you to seriously consider the message of this book. Yes, you will be entertained, inspired, and challenged, but never bored! *Set Yourself on Fire!* can transform your life because in plain language, engagingly written, Phil Taylor has unlocked great truths of life and living that will unshackle your chains and lead you to become fully alive.

Happy Journeys,
Dilip Abayasekara, Ph.D.
Former International President of Toastmasters International & Author of *The Path of the Genie: Your Journey to Your Heart's Desire*

1

WHAT ARE YOUR DREAMS?

"If one advances confidently in the direction of his dreams, and endeavors to live the life which he has imagined, he will meet with success unexpected in common hours."
—Henry David Thoreau

What are your dreams? Dreaming is fun, isn't it? But what if you could actually take your dreams and turn them into your reality? How awesome, empowering, and exhilarating would that be?

The fact of the matter is that only when we dream and pursue the very passions that are yearning to be set free do we fully become alive. Interestingly enough, not too long ago I was listening to an interview with actor Tom Selleck, who was recently inducted as an honorary member of the Horatio Alger Association. He spoke during the interview of his impoverished beginnings as a child growing up in Detroit. Also of the bold move that his parents took to go west to California to seek a better life, and the numerous stories of his struggles over the years as he progressively moved toward the achievement of his dreams. At the very end of the interview he said something very profound, which I will never forget. Verbatim, here is what he said: "Hopefully the kid in you will never die! That's where your dreams come from." And then with utmost sincerity and conviction he concluded by saying, "You know, I think when you stop dreaming, you start dying!"

For some reason that statement gave me the goose

bumps, as Tom Selleck confirmed what I was already so convinced about in my own heart.

First, he said, "Hopefully the kid in you will never die!"

This statement reminded me of a story I read years ago, in Bill Hybels's book *Who You Are When No One's Looking*, of a little boy who had such a dream.

It started like so many evenings. Mom and Dad were at home, and little Jimmy was playing after dinner. Both his parents were absorbed with jobs and did not notice the time. It was a full moon, and some of the light seeped through the windows.

Then Mom glanced at the clock. "Jimmy, it's time to go to bed! Go up now, and I'll come and settle you later."

Unlike usual, Jimmy went straight upstairs to his room. An hour or so later his mother came up to check if all was well, and to her astonishment found that her son was staring quietly out of his window at the moonlit scenery.

"What are you doing, Jimmy?"

"I'm looking at the moon, Mommy."

"Well, it's time to go to bed now."

As one reluctant boy settled down, he said, "Mommy, you know one day I'm going to walk on the moon!"

Who could have known? The boy, in whom this dream was planted that night, would survive a near fatal motorbike crash, which broke almost every bone in his body. But he would still bring to fruition his dream thirty-two years later when he, James Irwin, stepped on the moon's surface. He was just one of twelve representatives of the human race to have done so.

Set Yourself on Fire!

You see, James Irwin had a dream just like so many of us do, or did at one time. In his case, he held on tightly to his dream, believed in it fervently, and allowed the driving forces of faith and desire to bring to reality what many scoffed at.

We have but only a moment in the scope of eternity to seize the essence of what it means to truly be alive, don't we? And so the question becomes "What is your dream?" Did you once have a dream and for some reason or another the dream was lost, or some thoughtless individual stomped on it? The good news is, no matter what we've gone through and where we find ourselves at the present time, it is never, never too late to reignite the childlike faith and dreams that once burned so brightly within us as children.

Speaking about children, according to research from the University of Michigan, the average adult laughs only 15 times a day, but the average child laughs 150 times daily. That's ten times more than adults do! Not only did we dream more as children, but also we laughed more as well. I suppose it is a reflection of what Jesus said, when He called a little child and had him stand among his disciples: "I tell you the truth, unless you change and become like little children, you will never enter the kingdom of heaven" (Matthew 18:3).

Children have so much innocence and purity, don't they? And with these come wisdom, joy, and faith, and for some peculiar reason, all too often, they get lost as we grow into adulthood.

The second part of Tom Selleck's concluding statement was, "I think when you stop dreaming, you begin dying."

I don't quite know if Tom Selleck realized just how profound his two statements were, and that one day they would be studied and dissected in a book, like one attempts to unravel the mysteries of a great philosopher. On a side note, little did I ever expect to be analyzing the utterances of

Set Yourself on Fire!

Magnum P.I.! Emerson, Huxley, Thoreau, Shakespeare, yes! But, Magnum P.I.? Who would ever have known? However, all kidding put aside, those are pretty wonderful insights and profound words coming from this well-respected Hollywood actor. Wouldn't you agree?

I believe Tom Selleck hit the nail on the head when he stated the great importance of dreaming.

First, our dreams are powerful and beautiful because they often unveil the deep-seated desires of our hearts. In our dreams we can go anywhere, we can be anybody, and we can do anything. What if we can turn those dreams and make them reality?

Christopher Reeve once stated, "So many of our dreams at first seem impossible, then they seem improbable, and then when we summon the will, they soon become inevitable." If this is true, which I do believe it is, how important is it for us to hold on tight to our dreams?

Napoleon Hill, author and great researcher of some of history's greatest achievers, stated it in no uncertain terms when he wrote in *The Law of Success*, "Cherish your visions and your dreams as they are the children of your souls, the blueprints of your ultimate achievements."

Inevitably, if we desire to live the life that we so ardently desire, dreaming is where it all begins. All great accomplishments began in the form of a dream!

One of the greatest dreamers of our time was a young man from the Midwest who, after running out of money and consequently seeing his small business go bankrupt, still held on to his dream. Instead of giving up on his dreams, he packed up his suitcase with nothing but a few drawings, an unfinished product, $40 in his pocket, and then headed to California to start a new business.

Although he had to battle through much rejection and one adversity after another, he never stopped believing! Today, because he dared to tread in a time and place where no other man would even think of going, he left a lasting legacy and a gift to the world that warms the hearts of millions around the world. This great dreamer's name, perhaps you have heard of it, is none other than Walt Disney.

Interestingly enough, Walt Disney was notorious for challenging the limits of what was seemingly impossible. Walt would occasionally present some unbelievable, extensive dream he was entertaining. Almost without exception, the members of his board would gulp, blink, and stare back at him in disbelief, resisting even the thought of such a thing, but unless every member resisted the idea, Disney usually didn't pursue it. Why was that? Disney felt the challenge wasn't big enough to merit his time and creative energy, unless they were unanimously in disagreement.

Walt Disney used his dreams to spur himself onward. His ongoing mantra in life was, "If you could dream it, you could achieve it!"

It's interesting to note that researchers in the study of dreams agree that there is a purpose and importance to dreaming.

They discovered that people who are deprived from entering the dream phase of sleep, known as the REM stage, exhibit symptoms of irritability and anxiety. In one dream study, volunteers were woken up right before they entered into the dream state. Then they were allowed to fall back to sleep. And then they were woken up again, right before they entered REM sleep. Then again, they were allowed to fall back to sleep. And again, right before they entered REM sleep, they were woken up. This continued on through the night. The volunteers slept the same amount of time as they normally did. The next day, these volunteers went about their day. They were observed to be disoriented, depressed, crabby, and quick-tempered. There was a general impairment in their daily functioning. Some ate more than usual. As this study continued on through several nights, subjects became more and more noticeably agitated. Deprivation of REM sleep caused oversensitivity, lack of concentration, and memory loss.

This study showed the importance of dreaming and its role in our well-being and health. Some researchers believe dreams help us tackle stress. It is clear that dreaming helps to recharge the mind and revitalize the body. Extensive studies have uncovered that dreaming is not only a vital contributor to a healthy body and mind, but that dreaming is a necessity.

Over a century ago, the great poet and essayist Oliver Wendell Holmes expressed a sobering thought that reflects the human dilemma, even to this day, when he stated, "Many people die with their music still in them. Why is that?" He continued by explaining, "Too often it is because they are always getting ready to live. Before they know it, time runs out."

Too often we get caught up with the busyness of everyday life, and we forget what really means the most to us. Don't we? We become wandering generalities instead of meaningful specifics. Many of us stopped dreaming a long time ago, perhaps because someone whom we looked up to told us it wasn't possible.

For instance, I can remember, I must have been about seven years old. I loved playing baseball and going to games! One day I was in the driveway. I still can remember it as clear as yesterday, mostly because of how it made me feel. Excitedly, I informed my oldest brother that I was going to be a professional baseball player!

Cynically, he turned to me and said, "Oh, you could never be a professional baseball player; plus, you're too old!"

Too old, I silently exclaimed to myself, *I'm only seven!*

He went on to explain to me, "Kids who grow up to play in the big leagues have to start when they are two or three years old."

Set Yourself on Fire!

Well, since my brother was eleven years older than I was, and in my eyes he was infallible, I took what he said at face value. My heart sunk to my stomach, and right there and then—not knowing any better—I resigned to the notion that I could never achieve my dream of becoming a professional ballplayer.

I was always a dreamer. Looking back on my childhood I could remember numerous occasions when adults and teachers told me such things as I wasn't good enough, I couldn't spell, I was not capable of learning math or playing the piano, or even of capable of going to college.

As I look back today, I do so with a sense of chill at the hurtful and careless messages some trusted authority figures convey to children. In his book *What to Say, When You Talk to Yourself*, Shad Helmstetter states that before a person has reached the age of eighteen, on average he or she will have been told, "No!" or "You can't do it!" more than 148,000 times.

As a child in school, Thomas Edison had a hard time concentrating and would often get bored. He struggled in school and would come home with poor marks. His teacher called him "enable" (learning disabled). Consequently, Edison had only three months of formal education. Just imagine that! Dubbing Edison as learning disabled! Actually it was quite the opposite. Realizing and knowing this, his mother saw and understood the damaging consequences his schoolteacher could have on her young boy. His perceptive and wise mother pulled him out of school and decided to teach him from home. As it turned out, Edison proved to have a ferocious appetite for learning, forever asking questions, and getting his hands on everything he could read. History tells us the rest of his extensive and brilliant story. I wonder what was the name of his teacher? Could you imagine how history and our present day would be if Edison's mother took what his teacher said at face value? Thank goodness for wise and loving mothers! And yet, I often wonder just how many other Edisons in our history have fallen through the cracks because of the careless words of some less than competent authority figure.

It's no wonder that there is an ailment in our society that seems to repress people from being and going for what really lies within their hearts. Often, the conditioning of self-limitations was ingrained in our minds before we could even begin to really think for ourselves.

Perhaps it is for this reason, according to a study by Career Builder, that only one in five individuals in the continental United States and Canada is in a career that they truly love. According to similar studies, over 50 percent of all working individuals actually hate going to their place of work. In a society that arguably attests to the best lifestyle on earth, to have over 50 percent of the working population hate their jobs is one of the greatest tragedies of our time. Isn't life too short to be doing anything other than what is the expression of our true inner passion?

This dilemma can be traced way back to the negative messages of self-limitations, which so many people are told when growing up.

For the most part, as adults, in time we develop a filtering capability to assess what is true and what is not, in terms of what is conveyed to us. However, with children, it is not so. Children will readily believe what an adult tells them, and whether it is true or not, it will become part of their mind-set, and often they will carry it long into life.

It is for this reason that we must take extra care in how we talk to our children and teenagers. The messages we convey can and will have a profound effect on whether one grows up to be a happy, healthy, and fully functionally person, or one who lives in pain, well within the limits of one's own potential.

Although there is a phenomenon of self-limitation facing

our society, there is good news. And the good news is, no matter who we are or where we find ourselves in life, so long as there is breath in us, there is a guaranteed hope each one of us can begin to live the life we love, as of today, if we so choose! The key word in all of this is—"choose!"

It all begins with embracing a true perspective about who we are and what we possess. The seed of positive change begins with the right attitude.

The late Viktor Frankl was no stranger to adversity, and in what one might have considered the most hopeless of circumstances. During the Second World War, he, along with his newly beloved wife, father, mother, and brother, was captured by the Nazis and thrown into a concentration camp. By the time the war was over, he lost his family and every material possession he owned. However, he emerged from these unthinkable circumstances with one very powerful viewpoint on life, which could be encapsulated in this one powerful statement: "That everything can be lost to an individual except for one thing, the last of human freedoms, and that is the ability to choose one's attitude in any given set of circumstances."

Success and the pursuit of our dreams are cultivated in the soil of attitude—an attitude of faith in ourselves and our dreams. Without it, a dream can never be born. Attitude is the parent of all dreams.

Henry Ford was another great dreamer. Often criticized for his lofty dreams and seeming lack of education, he still pursued what people said was the impossible. But like Disney, Ford too had a mantra: "If you think you can, you can!" However, the flip side to the rest of his statement was, "If you think you can't, you're right." You can't!

While most people thought they couldn't, Ford thought and believed he could. Ford knew and experienced throughout his life the all-important, underlying power of the attitude of faith. Moreover, he never stopped pursuing what he believed was possible, simply because so-called experts told him that it couldn't be done.

Early in the age of the automobile, Ford decided to produce his now famous V-8 motor. He chose to build an engine with the entire eight cylinders cast in one block and instructed his engineers to produce a design for the engine. The design was put on paper, but every one of the engineers was convinced and agreed that it was simply an impossibility to cast an eight-cylinder gas engine block in one piece.

Ford said, "Produce it anyway."

"But," they replied, "it's impossible!"

"Go ahead," Ford commanded, "and stay on the job until you succeed no matter how much time is required." Six months went by, nothing happened. Another six months passed, and still nothing happened. The engineers tried every conceivable plan to carry out the orders, but the thing seemed out of the question—impossible!

At the end of the year Ford checked with his engineers, and again they informed him they had found no way to carry out his orders.

Ford left his engineers no option (save quitting him). And so they went on to tackle the task they thought impossible. They went ahead anyway, and then, as if by a stroke of magic, the secret was discovered.

Ford's unwavering attitude of faith had once again won out!

History is inundated with visionaries who rose above the average to dare great dreams to achieve the "impossible."

At a time when people thought the world was flat, Christopher Columbus had a dream of finding a new passage to the Orient by sailing west. In spite of the many personal attacks, criticisms, and doomsayers who said that the world was flat, and by going west he would sail off the face of the earth, Columbus held on tightly to his dream, pressed onward, and opened up a new world as we know it today.

At a time when the notion of flying in the open skies was

for the birds, Wilbur and Orville Wright dreamed that they could build an aircraft that would be capable of sustaining man. The Wright brothers had been fascinated by the idea of flight from an early age. It all started when their father gave them a flying toy made of cork and bamboo. It had a paper body and was powered by rubber bands. The young boys soon broke the fragile toy, but the memory of its faltering flight across their living room stayed with them. Captivated by this dream, they read every book and paper they could find on the still earthbound science of human flight. Methodically, step by step with faith, creativity, and perseverance, the Wright brothers finally realized their vision of powered human flight in 1903, which changed the course of history and forever made the world a smaller place.

At a time when the world was living more or less in the dark, Thomas Edison dreamed of creating a safe and inexpensive source of light that would be available to all. In spite of "trying and failing" over ten thousand times in his attempt to invent the incandescent lightbulb, his perseverance paid off; thanks to Edison, today we experience and see things in a new light.

At a time when long-distance communication was limited, Alexander Graham Bell dreamed of being able to create a device that would send human voice over a wire. He figured out how to transmit a simple current first, and then went out and received a patent for his invention on March 10, 1876. Three days later, he transmitted actual speech. Sitting in one room, he spoke into the phone to his assistant in another room, saying the now famous words: "Mr. Watson, come here! I need you!" As a result, the way of everyday communication and business was revolutionized, making way for a device that we have become dependent on, and which is used daily by billions around the world.

At a time when the Internet, e-mail, and instant messaging were something out of a science-fiction movie, Bill

Set Yourself on Fire!

Gates and his partner Paul Allen started Microsoft, dreaming big about software and an operating system that would be used by millions around the world. They envisioned the impact it could have. They talked about a computer on every desk and in every home. Today much of that dream has become a reality, and it affects countless lives in ways no one could have even imagined.

At a time when women were prohibited by law from voting, Susan B. Anthony dreamed of a nation where women would be treated with the same dignity, freedoms, and rights as men—a bold and revolutionary idea at the time. In November 1872, in Rochester, New York, she demanded to be registered and to be allowed to vote in the national election, only to be arrested shortly thereafter. In spite of being tried and found guilty, and having faced a lifetime of adversity, Susan Anthony never wavered from her vision. In the last speech she ever delivered, at a convention in Baltimore in February 1906, she was given a ten-minute ovation. In so many words, she told the women that the dream must not cease. In her parting words she appealed to her audience, "You must see that it does not stop. Failure is impossible." Although Susan Anthony died a month later, her dream lived on. Other women carried on her vision, and Congress passed the 19th Amendment of the U.S. Constitution, which the states ratified in 1920. The amendment states, "The right of a citizen of the United States to vote shall not be denied or abridged by the United States or any state on account of sex." One hundred years after she was born, Susan B. Anthony's dream was realized.

At a time of personal tragedy, just a month before her company was to begin operations, Mary Kay Ash's beloved husband suddenly died at the breakfast table, the victim of a heart attack. Heartbroken, she considered giving up on her dream. However, with strong encouragement from her family and with sheer determination, she pressed onward.

Set Yourself on Fire!

Having five thousand dollars of her personal savings set aside, a month later—on September 13, 1963, as originally planned—Mary Kay stood strong and launched her company. Although she came from meager beginnings, Mary Kay dared to dream big. As a result of her dream, Mary Kay was able to parlay a simple five-thousand-dollar investment into what became a $2 billion–plus company with 950,000 independent beauty consultants in thirty-five countries.

At a time when he was dismissed from his job as an assistant coach and strongly cautioned that he should not be coaching football, Lou Holtz found new hope that reignited his dream. For those of us who are sports buffs, the name Lou Holtz is a familiar one. Lou Holtz grew up in a household that loved the Notre Dame Fighting Irish football team. His grandfather, his father, and his uncles were big fans, and Lou inevitably inherited the feverish passion. He became greatly infatuated with the sport and the team.

He dreamed of one day becoming the head coach of the Notre Dame Fighting Irish. To some who may have overheard his aspirations, they might have dubbed him as delusional, to say the very least. In fact, early in his career, after being named assistant coach of the University of South Carolina football team, the head coach of the team was fired. The new incoming coach then dismissed Lou, cautioning him that maybe he shouldn't be coaching football.

Lou found himself devastated and unemployed. He had just spent the last of his money on a down payment for a home, and his wife was expecting the birth of their third child. It was during this time that his wife, in an attempt to lift his spirits, bought him a book by David Schwartz titled *The Magic of Thinking Big*. This book turned out to have a profound effect on Lou's life. After reading the book, he excitedly set out to list 107 items that he wanted to achieve in his lifetime. Included in his list were things that he wanted to be or do.

Set Yourself on Fire!

Among his wish list were a lot of fun and exciting action items, such as going down the Snake River, appearing on the *Tonight Show* with Johnny Carson, jumping out of a plane, having dinner at the White House, seeing the pope, and yes, even becoming head coach of the Notre Dame Fighting Irish!

As of the time of this writing, Lou Holtz has achieved 102 out of his 107 lifetime ambitions. Not only did he become head coach at Notre Dame, he did a remarkable job, taking a struggling team and restoring the Fighting Irish to the greatness to which it had once been accustomed. In addition, Lou Holtz is the only coach in NCAA history to lead six different programs to bowl games and the only coach to guide four different programs to the final top-20 rankings. He is also a multiple winner of the National Coach of the Year honors, and most fittingly, on May 1, 2008, Lou Holtz was elected to the College Football Hall of Fame. Not bad for a person who once was advised by a supposedly superior and more experienced coach that maybe, just maybe, he should not be coaching college football. Makes you wonder, doesn't it? Who was that guy who said that anyway?

In addition, it also makes one think: what would have ever happened if Lou Holtz had not picked up and read the powerful book that so profoundly impacted his life? Makes me think of what my late friend, Charlie "Tremendous" Jones, was so often quoted as saying: "You will be the same person in five years from now as you are today, except for two things, the people you meet and the books you read."

The list of achievers who took their dreams and made them a reality is exhaustive—too many to count. We can go on and on, one story after another, spelling out the achievements of individuals of today and of years gone by.

As we have been skimming over the biographies of some of the great achievers of history—be it in arts, science, literature, exploration, business, social reform, politics, or sports—one outstanding common denominator ties them all together. They all started with a dream, inspired by a burning passion within them to make that dream a reality—every one of them! No wonder the great German inventor and philosopher G. W. F. Hegel noted, "Nothing great has ever been accomplished without passion." Passion is the underlying essence that causes us to dream.

So the questions now become: "What is your true passion? What are your dreams? What would you do if there was no such thing as fear holding you back?" If you could do, live, and be anyone you wanted to, who would you be? What would that look like?

The fact of the matter is that as human beings we are only tapping into a very small percentage of our human capabilities—10 percent, at best, according to experts in the field of self-actualization. The difficulty for most people isn't that they can't achieve what they set out to be or do, but rather in not knowing their true calling and dreams in life.

As the old adage goes, "How can you score if you don't have a goal?"—that is, a dream with a specific action plan and a deadline for its achievement. As we go deeper into this book you will discover the very principles and steps required to turn your dream into reality. The exciting part is, if you can dream it, you are well on your way to living the life you love!

Finally, it seems only fitting that we conclude this chapter by giving due honor to one of the greatest dreamers in recent history.

On August 28, 1963, from the steps of the Lincoln Memorial in Washington, Martin Luther King Jr. set himself on fire by passionately declaring his dream to the world. During a period of great resistance and unthinkable conditions of racism and segregation, Martin Luther King Jr. articulated in descriptive detail his dream for a future where blacks and whites among others would coexist harmoniously as equals. This, at the time, was a tall order and, to many, an impossible dream.

However, so fervent was the expression of his dream that it forever set the course of positive change in American history, and ignited a momentum for equality that carries through to this day. Although this great dream came with the ultimate price that cost Martin Luther King Jr. his life, when he was assassinated in Memphis on April 4, 1968, his legacy and his dream live on.

If one mark defines greatness, it is when a person's dream exceeds one's own mortality. A great leader, a great person leaves the gift of the dream for generations to come. Martin Luther King Jr., as those who had gone before him—leaders such as Gandhi, Lincoln, and certainly Jesus Christ—paid the same price for their vision.

Did these men know that the price of their dreams would most likely cost them their lives? Absolutely! Knowing this, would they have changed anything? Not a thing! Martin Luther King Jr. put it in vivid terms when he stated, "If a man hasn't discovered something that he will die for, he isn't fit to live!"

A Point to Consider

"Hopefully the kid in you will never die. That's where your dreams come from."
—Tom Selleck

Questions to Ponder

1. What are your dreams?
2. What would you dare to dream if you knew you could not fail?

2

THE GREAT TRANSITION

"Make no little plans; they have no magic to stir men's blood and probably will themselves not be realized. Make big plans; aim high in hope and work, remembering that a noble, logical diagram once recorded will not die."
—Daniel H. Burnham

Could you imagine trying to build a house without a blue-print? What would the finished product look like, if it even ever was completed at all? Yet so many people go through life without giving much thought to planning their lives. According to numerous studies only 3 percent of the general population has ever taken the time and effort to clearly write down their life goals. Consequently, by the time most people reach the age of sixty-five, 95 percent of individuals are still not living their dream, and even worse, most find themselves dead broke. Imagine that: working in a job that you don't like most of your life, only to arrive at your golden years exhausted and broke. Is that a way to live? And yet these statistics lend credence to the old adage, "When you fail to plan, you plan to fail."

Oliver Wendell Holmes observed years ago that "the greatest tragedy in America is not the destruction of our natural resources, though that tragedy is great. The truly great tragedy is the destruction of our human resources by our failure to fully utilize our abilities, which means that most men and women go to their graves with their music still in them."

The sad truth is that most people spend more time planning out their vacations than they do planning out their lives.

If there was ever a time to plan out the life you love, and begin journeying toward the achievement of your dreams, it is now! The good news is that human beings are capable of achieving almost anything they put their minds to. The problem does not lie in inability, but rather in lack of clarity. Most people have not been able to identify their life goal, and if there is no goal, there is no plan. Others might know what they want, yet they fail to create a clear plan of action for its achievement; before they know it, their goal slips away from sight. Unless your dream is written down, it's only a wish. A goal is a goal, and it's within reach only when clearly written down and supported with a precise action plan for its achievement. What is your game plan for achieving your dream?

Before we examine the necessary procedures for achieving your goal, let's examine the reasons that most people fail to set goals.

Reason 1: Fear

So many people have been conditioned with the thought that setting goals is pointless, because over a period of time nothing good is going to happen to them anyhow. They have been told many times that they can't do things. Most of the input that people have received has been of a negative nature. As noted earlier, Shem Helmstetter, in his best-selling book *What You Say When You Talk to Yourself*, points out that the average person has been told, "No!" or "You can't do it," over 148,000 times by the age of eighteen. Moreover, studies have revealed that 77 percent of our self-talk and over 90 percent of our daily input is negative. Having received this negative conditioning, many people act on their self-defeating thoughts and don't even move off the starting line. The fear of failure has them beaten, even before they have given themselves a chance. "Why even try?" seems to be their dominating thought, and so they don't.

Another component to setting goals is it causes people to look at themselves and assess their own progress or lack of it. *What if I don't succeed?* they fearfully rationalize. They attach much pain to failure rather than viewing temporary setbacks as a necessary part of success. In an attempt to avoid this pain, they don't even bother trying, even if it means giving up on their dreams.

Reason 2: Poor Self-Image

Others don't set goals because they could not imagine in their wildest dreams deserving the wonderful and liberating gifts that await them in life. Psychologists have observed that people perform in accordance with the image they have of themselves. Reports show that most lottery winners lose, spend, squander, or give away all of their newfound money within a few years of winning it. Statistics show that 80 percent of lottery winners file bankruptcy within five years. The reason is that they failed to develop a millionaire's mind-set. As a result, they subconsciously re-create the reality that matches the image they have of themselves. They feel uncomfortable with so much money, so they find a way to get back to a reality that is consistent with their own self-image.

Reason 3. Not Realizing the Importance of Goals

If people really knew the vital importance and incredible power of goal setting, they would be doing it all the time and everywhere. However, many people have never been taught the importance of setting goals. Most individuals have heard about goal setting, but they don't realize the true power and value of it as a tool for success and high achievement. Perhaps they were never introduced to goal setting. After all, it is not something usually taught in our school system.

Moreover, many people shrug off setting out their goals. By getting caught up in the busyness of everyday life, they overlook the critical importance of goal setting. They ultimately become, as Zig Ziglar puts it, "wandering generalities" instead of "meaningful specifics."

I am always amazed at the number of well-intended individuals I come across on a regular basis who rationalize that they do not have time to set goals, when in reality it is the single most important aspect of all achievement! They say, "I'll set goals someday when things settle down a bit and I get more time," but they never end up finding the time.

In *What They Don't Teach You at Harvard Business School*, Mark McCormack cites a Harvard study conducted on students in the 1979 Harvard MBA program. Harvard MBA graduates were asked, "Have you set clear, written goals for your future and made plans to accomplish them?" Of the graduates willing to participate, 3 percent had written goals, 13 percent had goals but they had not written them down, and 84 percent had no specific goals.

Ten years later, the researchers followed up and found that the 13 percent with unwritten goals were making twice as much as the 84 percent with no goals, and the 3 percent with clear, written goals were making ten times as much as the other 97 percent combined!

Writing down your goals in printed form is essential for achievement. It provides a sense of direction, timing, and the exact knowhow needed to achieve your desired result.

Set Yourself on Fire!

Reason 4: Not Knowing How to Set Goals

Many people think they have goals, but what they really have are just wishes. You ask them what their goals are, and they say something vague and generic, such as, "I want to be rich," "I want a better job," or "I want to be healthy." Those are good dreams to have, but they are not goals.

Others say that they tried goal setting and concluded that it doesn't work. They tell you something along the lines of, "I tried setting a New Year's resolution a few years back, but I didn't even last a week!" What they don't realize is that most New Year's resolutions are merely vague wishes, not real goals. People almost never write them down or prepare a plan for achieving them.

Imagine someone trying to use a power drill without knowing that you have to plug it in, and then telling you the power drill doesn't work! Goal setting is a tool that helps you achieve what you want step by step, but you need to know how to use it properly or you won't get anything from it.

Setting Your Goals

So how do you go about mapping out your game plan? One of the wonderful aspects about goal setting is that it's not a complex process, but rather a simple and effective formula to achieving whatever you set out to do. Whether your goal lies in the area of your career, family, business, lifestyle, health and fitness, or a myriad of other areas of focus, you will discover that one effective formula works for all of them. This formula can be found in a simple seven-step process.

Set Yourself on Fire!

Step One: Identify clearly in documented form what you want to achieve.

Ironically the challenge with most people is not found in their inability to achieve their goals. Human beings are capable of achieving almost anything they set their hearts and minds to. The fundamental reason that most people do not reach the highest level of their capabilities isn't because they cannot; rather, in many cases, it is because most people do not know what it is they truly want. Even before they get started they are defeated, simply because they haven't clearly identified what they want. Knowing where you are going is the first and most fundamental part of goal achievement.

Step Two: Identify clearly the reason that you want to achieve your predetermined goal.

Providing the "why" in what we sent out to achieve is the very fuel that empowers an individual to persevere, particularly in moments of difficulty and adversity. The stronger the reason, the more strength you will have for the journey. So many of us, with the best of intentions, set out to achieve our goals. We get all excited, but days, weeks, or months later we lose focus, and our goals and dreams drift into the abyss. The reason is that we lose sight of the penetrating reason for pursuing our goal. For instance, if your goal was to win the Boston Marathon, undoubtedly this would require a lot of commitment and training. It would require that you get up at a certain time, often perhaps not in the best of weather conditions, and run every day. Certainly there would be days when staying in the warmth and comfort of your bedsheets might be an overwhelming temptation, or perhaps the distractions of friends or different eating patterns might pull you away from what you know you need to do in order to stay focused and fit. If the reason was not compellingly clear and mixed with strong emotions, it would be easy to fall into temptation. Would it not? But if your reason is always before you, and it is clear and powerful, it will give you the necessary energy you need to reach your goal.

Step Three. Identify the obstacles you need to overcome in order to reach your goal.

If one thing is for certain, any and all worthwhile goals and endeavors come with challenges that must be overcome. If that wasn't the case, everyone would be cruising along living exactly the life they love. However, that is not the case with most people, and one key reason is they haven't been able to uncover and address the challenges that stand between them and their dreams. Although some of the obstacles may come in the form of lack of money, physical challenges, or specific knowhow, most of the obstacles that stand in the way of people's accomplishments are purely mental. These obstacles are nothing more than self-limiting belief systems we have placed on ourselves. To reiterate what Henry Ford said, "If you think you can, or you think you can't, you're right!" Many of us struggle with low self-esteem, fears, and self-doubt that stand in the way of truly living our dreams. For instance, I've heard numerous stories of people who turned down promotions and jobs they really wanted, simply because the job required them to speak in public. Their fear obstructed their ability to enjoy a more prosperous and abundant quality of life. There are countless numbers of talented individuals who fail because they have allowed lack of focus, lack of discipline, and even certain addictions or habits to override their pursuit. What are the obstacles that are standing in the way of you and your success? Identify them, write them down, and move confidently toward overcoming whatever they may be.

Step Four. Identify the specialized knowledge you need in order to reach your goal.

Earl Nightingale, a famous radio broadcaster and author of *The Strangest Secret*, once said, "If you will spend an extra hour each day in study, in your chosen field, you will be a national expert in that field in five years or less." As individuals, we are inundated from an early age with all kinds of general knowledge; however, the individuals who know where they are going—and who are able to focus precisely on what they know they need to know in order to achieve their goals—are the ones who truly excel.

How does one acquire specialized knowledge? Either you teach it to yourself, or you hire the very best people you know in your area of need to guide you through. It is, though, preferable to learn a given skill yourself if you are able to. This is knowledge that, no matter what, can never be taken away from you and which empowers you for the rest of your life. As a wise individual, Lao Zi, once said, "If you give a man a fish, you feed him for a day; if you teach him to fish, you feed him for a lifetime." Now you should be asking yourself, *What specialized knowledge do I need in order to reach my goal?*

There are two ways to develop leverage through knowledge: become an expert in your chosen field of endeavor, and commit to knowing your product inside out.

Become an Expert

Resolve to become an expert in your chosen field of endeavor. Make a decision today to join the top 5 percent.

Read the best books in your field, and take every related course or seminar that will help you achieve this segment of your goal. Acquire, watch, and listen to every online program, DVD, or audio program in your chosen field of study. Become a lifetime learner, and immerse yourself in a never-ending quest for knowledge and self-improvement. Famed basketball coach Pat Riley once observed, "If you're not getting better, you're getting worse." Never stop your quest to become better at what you do.

Commit to Knowing Your Product Inside Out

Commit to knowing your product better than anyone else in your industry. By doing so, you will position yourself as the go-to guy or gal in your industry. When people think about your product or service, they will think of you. Just as Kleenex brand is to tissue, Coke is to cola, and FedEx is to courier services; your goal should be the same in the eyes of those whom you serve.

Finally, if for one reason or another you do not possess the specialized knowledge you need, acquire the knowledge by partnering up with the very best people in their given field of expertise. For instance, one such man was Henry Ford, who in spite of limited formal education had the business savvy to leverage his own strengths and leave the aspect of car manufacturing to others who had far more superior knowledge than he did. His keen ability to find, hire, and delegate the right people with the specialized knowledge carried the company to outstanding success. By knowing what he needed to acquire in a very focused and driven manner, he was able to achieve his goals. History is filled with great achievers who lacked the luxury of formal education, but had the keenness of mind to acquire, in whatever way possible, the specialized knowledge needed to succeed.

Set Yourself on Fire!

Step Five. Identify the people, places, and things you need to achieve your goal.

In an interview with Charlie Rose, Steve Jobs, the cofounder of Apple Computer, was asked what he thought of himself. Jobs responded by making sure he clarified the record on his success: "You know, the things that I have done in my life—I think the things that we do now at Pixar—these are team sports. They are not things that one person does. You have to have an extraordinary team because you are trying to climb a mountain with a whole party of people, a lot stuff to bring up the mountain. So one person can't do it!"

Contrary to perhaps popular perception, there is no such thing as a self-made man or woman. They all needed the cooperation and assistance of others to achieve their goals. Part of the whole process of mapping out your game plan is to identify the people, places, and things you will need to achieve your goal. What are they?

People

If, for instance, you wanted to start a home renovation business, some of the people you need to be part of your team may be skilled laborers. Consider who you want your customers to be. You might need to hire a salesperson or two, a web designer to create your website, a bookkeeper or accountant, and perhaps a finance person or a banker who will fund your startup. Who are the people you need on your team to make your dream come true?

Places

If you were to launch a consulting business, networking may be part of the mix of what you need to consider. You'd want to identify the places that yield the best results in terms of where you want to go. You may want to consider trade associations and shows within your industry, as well as places to network, such as Business Network International, Le Tip, Rotary, the Board of Trade, or Goal Achievers International. If your goal involves the need to augment your public speaking skills or simply overcome the fear of public speaking, you may want to join an organization like Toastmasters. Perhaps, a university course or two would give you a better understanding of a certain skill set. Whatever it may be, part of effective goal setting is to identify clearly the various places you need to go to progress toward your stated achievement.

Things

Finally, to make this phase of the goal planning process complete, consider the things you need to make your goal a reality. If, for instance, you are opening a retail store, you'd need to consider startup capital and how much? You'd need to find the right location, lighting, furnishing, supplies, cash register, computer, and inventory, to mention just a few items that would be on your list. What are the things you need in order to move confidently in the direction of your goal?

Set Yourself on Fire!

Step Six. Write down an action plan for the achievement of your goal.

Now that you have clearly identified your predetermined goal; exposed the obstacles you need to overcome; written down the specialized knowledge; and picked out the people, places, and things you need to achieve your goal, it's time to put in writing a definite action plan that will become your blueprint for success.

An effective way to do this is to start with your goal and work backward. Break your goal down into various time lines, including daily to-do lists, weekly goals, monthly targets, and yearly goals. For a free template on planning out your game plan, you can visit www.goalachievers.org and download the goal setting action planner.

Step Seven. Write down a time line for the achievement of each goal.

Writing down a date for when you will achieve your goal is so important, because it creates a sense of urgency and keeps you on track. Have you ever found yourself saying, *Someday I'll . . . someday I'll start exercising; someday I'll get to write that book; someday I'll join that organization; someday I'll buy that new house?* Writing down a deadline for the achievement of your predetermined goal takes you off of the "Someday Isle," and creates a definite time line as to when you will achieve your goal. A goal without a deadline is like playing a football or basketball game with no clock. It's endless, exhausting, and lacks the vital sense of direction and urgency needed to achieve your goal. An open-ended goal with no deadline is not a goal, but a wish!

Experts in the field of personal development have discovered that once a deadline for achievement is identified, both the conscious and subconscious mind go to work to finding ways to achieve the goal within the predetermined timeline. It's interesting to note that in the four quarters of a football game, statistics reveal that substantially more points are scored in the last quarter of the game than in any of the preceding three quarters. The reason? The team needs to reach the goal of winning within the allotted time frame, and they accelerate the process to do so. And so it is with the game of life and the timelines we set for ourselves. When there is a clear game plan and a definite time set for its achievement, goals are achieved!

Isn't it time to make the great transition—to start moving from the mere stage of wishing and hoping to actually putting yourself on the road toward achieving the life you love? What is your plan? As the famous adage goes, "If you fail to plan, you plan to fail."

Put your dream on paper. Write out in detail the seven steps that you need to achieve your dream. Your dream will then become your goal, and your goal will become your reality!

A Point to Consider

There is no such thing as a self-made man or woman. All successful individuals need the cooperation and assistance of others to achieve their goals.

Questions to Ponder

1. What obstacles do you need to overcome to reach your goal?
2. What action plan have you put in place for achieving your goal?

3

THE KEY THAT UNLOCKS THE DREAM

"If you think you can or you think you can't, you're right!"
—Henry Ford

They said it could not be done! However, on May 6, 1954, Roger Bannister did what no man could previously do.

Bannister, a runner, became the first man to break the four-minute-mile barrier—in 3 minutes and 59.4 seconds in England on a windy day. The media at that time called the breaking of the four-minute mile by Bannister one of the greatest athletic achievements of all time.

Prior to that day, it was commonly accepted that no man running could break the four-minute-mile barrier. It was commonly accepted as fact that the four-minute mile was a physical impossibility.

However, the reality was that the four-minute mile was only a psychological barrier.

Once Roger Bannister planted the thought in other runners through his achievement, it didn't take long for other athletes to join him. Within forty-six days, John Landy broke Bannister's record in 3 minutes and 57.9 seconds in Finland. By 1957, sixteen other runners had also broken the four-minute mile. Amazingly, it took forever up to 1954 for one man to achieve this great feat. Yet, within only three short years after that, sixteen other runners suddenly accomplished "the impossible."

The fact is that all too often what determines what we can

or cannot do is only a product of our own thinking. We limit ourselves through our own thinking, and by the same token we also can accomplish great things. As Henry Ford so vividly put it, "If you think you can or you think you can't, you're right!"

While everyone else believed that the four-minute mile was impossible, Bannister believed it was not impossible. This belief created this historic athletic breakthrough and paved the way for many others to achieve the same.

As we analyze the lives of remarkable achievers, we see that they all start off with a dream and transform that dream into a clear, workable goal, but also back up their dream and goal with a strong belief—that whatever they conceive, believe, and aim toward, they can ultimately achieve!

Faith is the very key that turns on the propelling power of our dreams. Henry David Thoreau clearly identified this element of faith when he wrote the inspiring and powerful words, "If one advances confidently in the direction of his dreams, and endeavors to live the life which he has imagined, he will meet with success unexpected in common hours." The key point to highlight in this incredible statement is the word "confidently." It is a confidence that can only be produced as a result of a deep-seated belief.

Before we delve deeper into the principle of faith, an essential requirement for all achievement, it may be helpful to examine what faith is not.

Hands down, the biggest killer of dreams is found in the very opposite of the definition of faith, and that is fear and doubt.

Fear is dangerous, and it erodes any chances for individuals to achieve success. More than any other force out there, this toxic essence has been the source that has stopped people from moving forward and achieving their dreams. There are four major reasons that fear must be conquered.

Set Yourself on Fire!

Reason One: Fear Cripples Us from Moving Forward

In an article in *Today in the Word*, there was an account written about a man who hid for thirty-two years fearing punishment of pro-Nazi wartime activity. He said that he used to cry when he heard happy voices outside, but dared not show himself, even at his mother's funeral. Janez Rus was a young shoemaker when he went into hiding at his sister's farmhouse in June 1945. He was found years later, after she bought a large supply of bread in the nearby village of Zalna. "If I had not been discovered, I would have remained in hiding. So I am happy that this happened," Rus told a reporter. Throughout that time, he did nothing. He never left the house, and he could only look down at the village in the valley below. To him the fear was very real, and understandably so; however, the reality was very different. Fear had sent him into hiding and robbed him of thirty-two years of living.

Reason Two: Fear Contributes to Poor Health

Dr. E. Stanley Jones wrote in *Transformed by Thorns*, about a Johns Hopkins University doctor who said, "We do not know why it is that worriers die sooner than the non-worriers, but that is a fact." Jones thought he had the answer. He wrote that "we are inwardly constructed in nerve and tissue, brain cell and soul, for faith and not for fear. To live by worry is to live against reality."

Reason Three: Fear Is Irrational and Is a Useless Energy Drain

One study, reported on in the *Protection Connection*, showed that an average person's anxiety is distributed as follows:

40% on things that will never happen.
30% on things about the past that can't be changed.
12% related to criticism by others, mostly untrue.
10% on health, which gets worse with stress.
8% on real problems that will be faced.

Reason Four: Fear Produces Negative Thinking and Thus Fosters Negative Results

A humorous story illustrates this point about fear. Perhaps some of us have experienced a similar situation. James Hewett included this story in *Illustrations Unlimited*:

> When you fear that the worst will happen, your own thoughts may help to bring it about. "Fear," a writer once said, "is the wrong use of imagination. It is anticipating the worst, not the best that can happen."
>
> A salesman, driving on a lonely country road one dark and rainy night, had a flat. He opened the trunk—no lug wrench. The light from a farmhouse could be seen dimly up the road. He set out on foot through the driving rain. Surely the farmer would have a lug wrench he could borrow, he thought. Of course, it was late at night—the farmer would be asleep in his warm, dry bed. Maybe he wouldn't answer the door. And even if he did, he'd be angry at being awakened in the middle of the night. The salesman, picking his way blindly in the dark, stumbled on. By now his shoes and clothing were soaked. Even if the farmer did answer his knock, he would probably shout something like, "What's the big idea waking me up at this hour?"
>
> This thought makes the salesman angry. What right did that farmer have to refuse him the loan of a

lug wrench? After all, here he was stranded in the middle of nowhere, soaked to the skin. The farmer was a selfish clod—no doubt about that! The salesman finally reached the house, and banged loudly on the door. A light went on inside, and a window opened above.

"Who is it?" a voice called out.

"You know who it is," yelled the salesman, his face white with anger. "It's me! You can keep your blasted lug wrench. I wouldn't borrow it now if you had the last one on earth!"

The point is that fear produces all sorts of negativity and limited thinking and behaviors. The reality is that fear is a very real and very broad sensation known to humankind that can take many different shapes and forms. What may seem ridiculous to some may be very real to others. There are all sorts of fears, and all of them, no matter what, can be debilitating.

Dale Carnegie, in his best-selling book *How to Stop Worrying and Start Living*, noted that human beings are not creatures of logic, but beings that bristle with all kinds of fears and prejudices.

When one considers the vast array of fears that some people are obsessed with, it is not difficult to understand what he was saying.

Some fears are not so uncommon:

Acrophobia—fear of heights
Claustrophobia—fear of confined spaces
Mysophobia—fear of being contaminated with dirt or germs
Necrophobia—fear of death
Agoraphobia—fear of overcrowded places
Aviophobia—fear of flying
Carcinophobia—fear of cancer

And, well, the list goes on and on. These fears might seem ridiculous to some, but to others they are very real.

Certain other fears can really deal a direct blow to one's ability to succeed:

Kakaorrhaphiophobia—fear of failure or defeat
Atelophobia—fear of imperfection
Neophobia—fear of new things
Decidophobia—fear of making decisions
Anthropophobia—fear of people or society
Catagelophobia—fear of being ridiculed
Logizomechanophobia—fear of computers
Peniaphobia—fear of poverty
Prosophobia—fear of progress
And, if that isn't enough, there is even
Phronemophobia—fear of thinking!

Now, if I may say so, that's not a real good head space to be in, particularly if one wants to achieve goals and dreams!

Then there is the most common fear of all. In fact, according to *The Book of Lists*, this fear affects 75 percent of people to one degree or another. What is it? Glossophobia—the fear of public speaking, also informally referred to as stage fright.

Extensive research confirms the fact that the biggest fear known to human beings is the fear of public speaking. This fear is greater than the fear of heights, the fear of sickness, and even the fear of death. Comedian Jerry Seinfeld remarked, "According to studies, people's number-one fear is public speaking. Number two is death. Death is number two? Does that seem right? That means that to the average person, if you go to a funeral, you're better being in the casket than doing the eulogy!" Well, he has a point; it certainly puts things into perspective, doesn't it?

I mention this because I, too, could relate to the enormous fear that can overtake an individual when called upon to speak in public, and ultimately the frustration, sense of low self-esteem, and pain that results from this fear. Moreover, it robbed me from my dreams and all sorts of opportunities. This dragon of fear had me licked! I was hoping and thinking, one day, somehow, I would miraculously wake up and the fear would no longer be there. Nothing was further from the truth; in fact, the very opposite occurred. With every refusal to confront this fear, and every year that went by, my fear grew bigger and bigger until it translated itself into a literal sense of terror. For almost twenty long years, I lived within the grips of this terrible fear. It wasn't until the pain and lost opportunities became so great, as a result of my phobia, that I took the determined action steps to slay this dragon. To my astonishment I discovered that the very thing that had so much control over my life, which had robbed me from pursuing my dreams, was only a figment of my imagination. It wasn't real. It felt real, it appeared real, but it wasn't real! It reminds me of one definition for F-E-A-R: False Evidence Appearing Real. I cringe when I think of the countless opportunities and joy that were forfeited over the years because of my fear. The good news is that because of simply doing what I feared most, the fear disappeared, and I no longer live in the stranglehold of this fear. As a result, I can pursue my dreams with freedom and joy!

Whatever our fears might be, we must move beyond them if we are going to live an empowered life.

How to Overcome Fear

So how does one overcome this self-limiting sensation we call fear? The answer is so basically simple that it may astound you. Do what you fear most, and fear will disappear! Do you feel sick or nervous about something? Just do it! Look fear straight in the face, take out your metaphorical sword of faith, and slay that dragon! It's that simple.

Either you conquer fear, or fear conquers you. The choice is yours. Once you exercise courage, you'll feel empowered. Your spirit will be lifted, and you will discover a newfound freedom and energy to pursue your dreams.

If you haven't done so already, one day you will learn to welcome fear, because with fear comes opportunity—an opportunity to exercise courage, an opportunity to break away from your comfort zone, and an opportunity to grow like you never have done before!

This liberating insight can be best illustrated by Hannah Hurnard, author of *Hinds' Feet on High Places*, who also at one time was paralyzed by fear. Then she heard a sermon on scarecrows that challenged her to turn her fear into faith.

> The preacher said, "A wise bird knows that a scarecrow is simply an advertisement. It announces that some very juicy and delicious fruit is to be had for the picking. There are scarecrows in all the best gardens. If I am wise, I too shall treat the scarecrow as though it were an invitation. Every giant in the way, which makes me feel like a grasshopper, is only a scarecrow beckoning me to God's richest blessings." He concluded, "Faith is a bird which loves to perch on scarecrows. All our fears are groundless."

The Bible declares that "God has not given us the spirit of fear; but of power, and of love, and of a sound mind" (2 Timothy 1:7). That's a far cry from the diverse fears many of us face throughout our lifetime.

King Solomon ages ago wrote, "There is no need to panic over alarms or surprises, or predictions that doomsday's just around the corner, because God will be right there with you; He'll keep you safe and sound" (Proverbs 3:25).

This faith in a loving God, who only wants the very best for us, can clear our minds and hearts so that we can pursue a truly purposeful, empowering, and meaningful life.

Faith Defined

So now that we have examined what faith isn't, we turn to what faith is.

The *American Heritage Dictionary* defines faith as a confident belief in the truth, value, or trustworthiness of a person, idea, or thing. Faith is a belief that does not rest on logical proof or material evidence.

Now that's faith! One could even say that it takes faith to have faith.

The extraordinary beauty and dynamism of faith is that one will discover the truth and the wondrous and almost unexplainable mysteries that govern the universe, once faith is applied.

We have all heard the expression, "I'll believe it when I see it!" However, this is the way of the skeptic, the naysayer. The sad truth is that you'll never see a person who is negative achieve anything of any significance. But the true achiever, the dream maker, knows very well that if he can first believe it, he will then see it. Faith comes before matter. Faith is what unlocks a mere thought, a dream, and brings it into fruition.

The reality is that it takes faith to do anything. If one does not have faith, whether it be big or small, he or she will remain absent from the fulfillment and experiences of life. For instance, if you want to fly from New York to Los Angeles, but for some reason do not believe that the plane could sustain you in the skies, you'll never get on the plane. You'll never experience what it means to fly.

Despite the indisputable evidence, though we may not

fully understand the integral mechanics of how a plane works, most of us, by faith, are able to get on a plane and trust that it will. However, there are those who, for one reason or another, fear flying and would never get on a plane. Their lack of faith prevents them from the experience and the benefits of flying.

So it is with everything in life. It takes faith to move forward. We sit on a chair because we believe the chair will hold us up. We drive on a two-way highway because we believe that the oncoming car will not crash into ours. We put our money in the bank because we believe that the bank is trustworthy with our money. If we didn't have a degree of faith, we simply wouldn't do any of those things. The truth of the matter is that there are few people who won't do any of those things simply because they do not believe.

These are simple examples of faith. One may argue, well, it doesn't take much faith to do any of those things. I would agree. The point is, however, that our experiences in life will be in direct proportion to our faith. There are some people who have extraordinary faith, and sure enough, extraordinary things happen to them.

The Gospel of Matthew tells of an account where two blind men followed Jesus pleading for mercy and pity. After they entered a house the two blind men came to Him and Jesus asked them, "'Do you believe that I could do this?'

"'Yes, Lord,' they replied.

"Then he touched their eyes, saying, 'According to your faith, will it be done to you.' And their sight was restored" (Matthew 9:28–29).

It was an extraordinary miracle, by people with an extraordinary faith. History is filled with incidences and miracles that cannot be explained by medical science and can only be credited to one's faith.

Before the advent of the Alcoholics Anonymous 12-step program, it was a widely accepted notion that there was little to no hope for the alcoholic to overcome the deadly disease of alcoholism, outside of an occasionally rare and extraordinary spiritual experience. On June 10, 1935, two men who shared the same ailment founded an extraordinary movement called Alcoholics Anonymous, whose precepts were built entirely on faith. The irony is, where the science of medical advancement had failed and could do little to effectively address the deadly disease of alcoholism, faith took over, and it has dumbfounded the medical science field ever since. Today as a result of this faith, there are almost 2 million members of Alcoholics Anonymous, with over one hundred thousand groups worldwide. No other alcohol treatment program in the world has come remotely close to the success rate found among these individuals of faith. Ask a member who has found relief from the disease through this program, and that person will say with utmost sincerity that their experience is nothing short of a miracle! Faith works.

So powerful and extraordinary is this phenomenon of faith that this 12-step program has been adopted by myriad different support groups around the world that specialize in empowering individuals to overcome their particular ailments.

So how does all this happen? I believe Augustine expressed it well when he wrote, "Faith is to believe what we do not see, and the reward of faith is to see what we believe." In other words, believe it, and you will achieve it! As much as it is in the measure of your faith, so it will be done unto you.

By now you might be asking yourself, *How does this apply to my life and my dreams?* The answer is simple. It takes faith to move forward; it takes faith to ignite a dream and turn it into its reality. If you study success stories, you will discover another string of commonality that runs through every story; they were all men and women of faith.

They had faith in their dreams, faith in their abilities, faith in their colleagues, and in many cases they had faith in God.

Set Yourself on Fire!

For those who put their faith in God, it was relatively simple to achieve their goals. For they believed and knew God could and would do for them what they could not do for themselves. They believed, as it is written in the scriptures of old, "With God all things are possible!" (Matthew 19:26). And so they became possibility thinkers. Saint Paul was one of these great possibility thinkers, declaring in no uncertain terms, "I can do all things through Christ which strengthened me" (Philippians 4:13). And so equipped with this great faith, he dared to do great things, and he did!

The wonderful element about a faith in the Almighty God is that it supersedes the limitations of human thinking. Where man says it's impossible; the Almighty intervenes and boldly declares, "With God all things are possible!" Theologian George Fredrick Muller once noted, "Faith does not operate in the realm of the possible. There is no glory for God in that which is humanly possible. Faith begins where man's power ends."

Individuals can accomplish great things in and of themselves. However, if people take that faith and place it in a power greater than themselves, they will see and experience things of supernatural proportions that cannot even be explained. The greater your faith, the greater your achievements.

King Solomon was the most extraordinary leader of his day. People were in complete awe over his wisdom, power, and enormous success. He was the richest and most successful man of his era. Everything he touched seemed to turn to gold. When he wrote the book of Proverbs almost three thousand years ago, he shared the secret of his success. It was deeply seated in faith. What was his secret? "Trust in God from the bottom of your heart" (Proverbs 3:5).

It's interesting to note that while on earth the most frequent thing Jesus kept telling his disciples was, "Fear not, don't be afraid." He knew that fear was a natural tendency for human beings. He also knew the essential need and power of embracing faith.

It would be remiss to write this book and not acknowledge the source of true achievement. One thing is certain: all truly successful individuals were people of faith. America was founded on faith. It is no accident that we find written on U.S. currency, "In God We Trust." That is quite a statement, with a profound meaning!

The founding fathers of America were men of faith. George Washington, the first president of the United States, was a man of faith. The great entrepreneurs of the industrial revolution, such as Rockefeller, Carnegie, and Edison, all the way through to more contemporary figures, such as Martin Luther King Jr., Mary Kay Ash, and Lou Holtz, to Canadian billionaire Jimmy Pattison, were and are all individuals of faith. Yes, they believed in their dreams, they believed in themselves, they believed in others, and most important, they believed in an infinite source of power that comes only from God—a God that defined their values, attitudes, and principles, guiding them to extraordinary success. Faith is central to every great person's success, whether each person chooses to share it publicly or not. Faith is there.

This chapter is not intended or designed to go into a deep analytical observation of who God is. It merely points out that people who achieved significant success are people who possess great faith. The more authentic the source of their faith, the more successful is their endeavor. Show me a person of faith, deep faith, and I'll show you someone who is strong, happy, superpositive, and resilient—a person, shall we say, who has truly set herself or himself on fire! Show me a person, on the other hand, who is skeptical and full of doubt, and I'll show you a person who is afraid, negative, unhappy, and sadly limited by a lack of faith.

Your ability to achieve your dreams is in direct proportion to your faith. The more authentic your faith, the more authentic will be your experience and the ultimate achievement of your dreams.

There is one thing for certain: faith and fear cannot coexist. Either faith or fear controls your life. The greatness of faith is that just as light extinguishes darkness, so does faith extinguish fear.

May I suggest and encourage you to have faith in your dreams, faith in your abilities, faith in those you work with, faith in the wondrous laws that govern this universe, and most important, faith in God.

The more faith you have, the more empowered you will become. It will provide you with the confidence, the joy, and the strength to move mountains!

How to Cultivate Faith

Finally, now that we've examined the paramount importance and power of faith, the question becomes, "How does one cultivate and nurture faith?"

The first step is to recognize that faith is the product of the mind. Realizing what we allow in our minds, whether it is negative or positive, will have a profound effect in the way we think, believe, and act.

Ancient writings have declared that as a person thinks, so he or she is (Proverbs 23:7). Earl Nightingale in his best-selling book referred to this principle as *The Strangest Secret*. "We become what we think of most. Whatever we think about most expands, and we inevitably attract whatever we hold in our minds. It is one of the great laws of the universe, whether we fully understand it or not. Just like the law of gravity, we may not fully understand it; some do, and some people don't. I sure don't. But one thing I do know for certain is that it does exist, whether I like it or not. One can argue against it. However, it will still be what it is. So it is with this law that governs our thoughts."

Napoleon Hill, author of *Think and Grow Rich*, remarked that one of the very wonderful gifts endowed to us from our creator is the ability to choose our thoughts. We have the power to control our thoughts.

If we expose our minds to fear, we foster negativity, and with negativity we cripple our abilities to move forward in a bright, positive matter. However, if we dwell on, meditate on, and expose ourselves to bright, hopeful, and positive people, thoughts, and things, this, too, will expand. Our lives are a manifestation of our thoughts. Faith produces love, and love produces faith. They feed off each other, and these virtues set off an increasing amount of life-enhancing sparks: sparks of hope, goodness, wisdom, trust, perseverance, kindness, understanding, and joy.

For this reason, Saint Paul exhorted his readers to dwell upon, "Whatever is true, whatever is noble, whatever is right, whatever is pure, whatever is lovely, whatever is admirable—if anything is excellent or praiseworthy—think about such things" (Philippians 4:8). He knew and understood the power of the mind.

King Solomon wrote, "Guard your heart above all else, for it determines the course of your life" (Proverbs 4:23). If we allow toxic thoughts to enter our mind and heart, toxic words and behaviors will come out of our lives. Again, it's an old adage that declares, "Garbage in! Garbage out!" On the other hand, if we welcome empowering thoughts into our minds, empowering actions and behaviors will naturally flow out of our lives. Yes, it is the strangest secret, but it's true.

We cultivate faith from what we place in our minds. The more positive input we give it, the more our faith grows. And as our faith grows, we begin to experience its manifestation. As we experience its manifestation, our faith grows even stronger, and with this faith, we are energized with insight and strength to achieve our dreams.

Set Yourself on Fire!

Faith is essential. Faith is what determines whether you achieve that which you set out to do or not. In simple terms, if you believe you can, you can; if you believe you can't, you won't. When Roger Bannister achieved the four-minute mile, the only thing that made the difference between his success and those who did not succeed was that he believed. And so it is with every great achievement in history: it was propelled by a profound, unwavering faith.

Napoleon Hill said it best when he stated, "Whatever the mind of man can conceive and believe, it can achieve!"

It first takes a dream. And then it takes a faith to achieve that dream! Do you have that faith?

What will you do today to begin cultivating and nurturing that all-important attitude of faith?

A Point to Consider

Faith and fear cannot coexist. Either faith or fear is in charge of your life.

Questions to Ponder

1. What fears, if any, are standing between you and your success?
2. What will you do today to begin cultivating and nurturing that all-important attitude of faith?

4

JUST DO IT!

"Dreams pass into reality of action. From the actions stems the dream again; and this interdependence produces the highest form of living."
—Anais Nin

The May 1991 issue of *Pulpit Helps* includes the following story:

"Dr. J. B. Gambrel tells an amusing story from General Stonewall Jackson's famous valley campaign. Jackson's army found itself on one side of a river when it needed to be on the other side. After telling his engineers to plan and build a bridge so the army could cross, he called his wagon master in to tell him that it was urgent the wagon train cross the river as soon as possible. The wagon master started gathering all the logs, rocks and fence rails he could find and built a bridge. Long before daylight General Jackson was told by his wagon master all the wagons and artillery had crossed the river. General Jackson asked 'Where are the engineers and what are they doing?' The wagon master's only reply was that they were in their tent drawing up plans for a bridge."

Now that you have identified your dream, laid out a practical plan of action, and are fueled with a deep-seated faith for its achievement, it's time to go to work. However, when you are following your heart, it's not really work, but a feverish labor of love that fuels you onward. The key is to never lose sight of your goal and to take continual, definite action until your dream is realized.

Following your dreams is exciting! Translating your dreams into concrete plans is vital. Having your dreams energized with faith is essential. Having said all of that, there is no substitute for the supreme ingredient of action. All the dreaming and all the planning in the world are futile, unless they are backed up with action!

However, it seems that some people are forever dreaming and planning and never taking action.

Do you know anyone like that? Those, "bless their hearts," who are always planning, but never doing?

Let's face it. Our dreams are empty, our plans lie in the dust, and our goals go nowhere unless they are followed through with action.

It may be of interest to note that most people after attending a seminar, reading an inspirational book, or listening to a motivational audio program never take action on what they have learned. Moreover, statistics indicate that two-thirds of people who purchase self-improvement products never even finish reading or even listen to them. Consequently, their lifestyle does not improve.

Perhaps for this reason Herbert Spencer noted, "The great aim of education is not knowledge but action!"

There is no point in education if one does not put what is learned into action. Knowledge without action is useless.

Before we delve into the importance of taking action, let us look at the three fundamental reasons that many individuals fail to take action.

Reason One: Lack of Preparation

An ancient philosopher stated, "Success depends upon

previous preparation, and without such preparation there is sure to be failure."

Many individuals get swept away by the promise of what a particular audio program book or seminar can deliver. They purchase the product or ticket to the event and then simply show up on the day, but they haven't thought through what it is they specifically want to get from their educational investment.

When it comes to seminars, all too often people show up without even a pen or pencil and something to take notes on.

Glenn Dietzel, author of *Author and Grow Rich*, says, "Writing is the doing part of thinking."

If individuals are not prepared to even take notes, what hope is there that they will take action after the event?

When it comes to reading, I've always found it helpful to read a book with a pen and highlighter, continually highlighting the sentences and making notes on information that can and will be useful.

Decide beforehand what you want to gain from your educational investment in a book or a seminar. Be actively on the lookout for that one jewel of transformational insight.

When attending seminars, maybe your objective is to seek new information about a particular topic, or perhaps you may want to network and gain new business contacts. You might even want the opportunity to have a one-on-one discussion with the presenter. Decide the best way to achieve what you want.

Be prepared to take notes. Have a list of questions to which you're seeking answers, and have a large stack of business cards to share.

Remember, the more prepared you are, the more professional you'll come across, and the more you'll gain from the event.

Set Yourself on Fire!

Reason Two: Lack of Belief

Stuart Chase stated, "For those who believe, no proof is necessary. For those who don't believe, no proof is possible."

Every now and then, speakers begin their presentation with the words, "Don't believe a word I say." They mean it sincerely as they are asking you to question and challenge what you hear from them, as opposed to just soaking it all in. They are asking you to listen to what they have to say and then come to your own conclusions. When your mind is in such a questioning state, you are more attentive and you tend to remember more of what has been said.

However, our subconscious mind does not process negatives, so to the subconscious mind, the initial instruction effectively comes across as, "Believe every word I say."

Still, some people are very skeptical. Perhaps they were somehow coerced into attending the event and thus they become unwilling participants. They see the speaker as a charlatan, and they are ready to pick holes in whatever the speaker says. They close their mind to learning new knowledge, and needless to say, they are definitely in no mood for taking action after the event.

Sometimes attendees lack self-belief. They listen avidly to the presentations, but deep inside they don't believe that they can achieve the level of success that the speaker has achieved. They forget or close their minds to the fact that many of the speakers came from very humble origins. They forget that the journey to success for many of these individuals was a painstaking journey, comprising many years.

Some of these individuals have good intentions, but after the seminar they will sabotage all their efforts to follow through.

Set Yourself on Fire!

Reason Three: A Sense of Being Overwhelmed

Mark Twain said, "The secret of getting ahead is getting started. The secret of getting started is breaking your complex and overwhelming tasks into small manageable tasks, and then starting on the first one."

Many seminars nowadays, in order to provide value for money and to appease a wide range of appetites, present a lineup of speakers. Sometimes you can hear as many as twelve speakers over the course of a weekend, all speaking on different topics.

You'll have the opportunity to witness some stunning presentations and hear some amazing information. You are blown away. Most of the speakers will have a program that they'll invite you to purchase, and I've seen some individuals buy a truckload of programs.

The trouble is that there is no way a person can do justice to all these programs. They get into a state of being completely overwhelmed, and they end up doing little or nothing. The programs get shelved, and maybe even get packed away in the garage where they gather dust and are forgotten.

When you go to a seminar, check out who is presenting and what they will be speaking about. Prioritize the speakers you most want to hear and what you want to learn from them. It's fine to listen and learn from the other speakers as well, but it may be wise to refrain from being pulled in too many different directions.

The hallmark of success is focus! It may be that you could incorporate all the different strategies you hear or read into your business, but you'll never be able to do this all at once. Decide what is important or even what you think you can handle at this time. Phase things in gradually.

The important thing is to gain some measure of success as efficiently as you can. There's nothing like that feeling of success when your hard work starts to pay off. You can then build on that success.

The Critical Importance of Follow-Through

In Napoleon Hill's best-selling book *Think and Grow Rich*, he relates the story of R. U. Darby's uncle, who was caught by the fever in the gold-rush days and went west to dig himself into a fortune. Staking his claim, he went to work with pick and shovel. The going was hard, but his determination to find gold was definite. As the story is told, his hard labor was rewarded by the discovery of the shining ore. He needed machinery to bring the ore to surface. Quietly, he covered up the mine and went back to his home in Williamsburg, Maryland, to tell his relatives and a few friends of his exciting discovery. Seizing the opportunity, they got money together for the needed machinery and had it shipped to Colorado. Darby and his uncle then went back to work the mine.

As the story is told, the first car of ore was mined and shipped to a smelter, which confirmed they had uncovered one of the richest mines in the state. A few more cars of ore would clear their debts; then the enormous profits would come.

As they kept drilling with great hope and anticipation, something happened! The vein of gold had disappeared! They had come to the end of the rainbow, and the pot of gold was nowhere to be found. Desperately they kept on drilling in an attempt to pick up the vein, but to no avail.

Finally, in exasperation they decided to quit. They sold the machinery to a local junk man for a few hundred dollars and went back home. However, the junk man who purchased the machinery had the sense to call in a mining engineer to take a second look at the project and do a little calculating. The engineer advised that the project had failed because the Darbys were not familiar with fault lines. His investigation showed that the vein of gold would be found just three feet from where the Darbys had stopped drilling. That is precisely where it was found.

The junk man took millions of dollars in ore from the mine, while Darby and his crew went back home broke. R. U. Darby was eventually able to pay back every dollar that he had borrowed from friends and relatives, although it took him years to do so.

More important, remembering that he lost a huge fortune because he had stopped three feet from the goal, Darby had profited from the experience by vowing that he would never repeat the same mistake. As he endeavored into a new career in life insurance, he reminded himself by saying, "I stopped three feet from gold, but I will never stop because men say 'No!' when I ask them to buy insurance."

As a result, Darby went on to make a fortune in his chosen field of endeavor. He owes his "stick ability" to the lesson he learned from his "quit ability" in the gold mining business.

Before success comes to anyone's life, he or she is sure to meet with much temporary defeat, and perhaps some failure. When defeat overtakes an individual, the easiest and most logical thing to do is to quit. That is exactly what the majority of people do.

As it has often been noted, "It is always darkest before the dawn."

If you study the lives of successful people, you will discover more often than not, as Hill wrote, "Their greatest success came to them just one step beyond the point at which defeat would have overtaken them."

One of the principal keys to success is "never quit." As Vince Lombardi said, "Winners never quit, and quitters never win!" The ability to persevere in times of great challenges is what makes the difference between success and failure.

Perseverance Is at the Heart of Action

The *Random House Dictionary* describes perseverance as a "steady persistence in a course of action, a purpose, a state, in spite of difficulties, obstacles, or discouragement."

Every champion athlete is certainly well acquainted with the essential ingredient of perseverance. In *The Book of Lists*, Quandt and Wallace wrote, "During a Monday night football game between the Chicago Bears and the New York Giants, one of the announcers observed that Walter Payton, the Bears' running back, had accumulated over nine miles in career rushing yardage. The other announcer remarked, 'Yeah, and that's with somebody knocking him down every 4.6 yards!' Walter Payton was inducted into the prestigious National Football League Hall of Fame, and goes down in history as one of the most successful running backs ever. He knew that everyone, even the very best, gets knocked down. He was very aware that the key to success is to get up and run again just as hard."

Three-time Olympic gold medalist Wilma Rudolph certainly understood the power of perseverance. According to an article in the Moody Bible Institute's *Today in the Word*, "Wilma didn't get much of a head start in life. She had a bout with polio, her left leg was crooked and her foot twisted inward, and she had to wear leg braces for much of her young life. After seven years of painful therapy, she could walk without her braces. At age twelve, Wilma tried out for a girl's basketball team, but didn't make it. Determined, she practiced with a girlfriend and two boys every day. The next year she made the team. When a college track coach saw her during a game, he talked her into letting him train her as a runner. By age fourteen, she had outrun the fastest sprinters in the U.S. In 1956, Wilma made the U.S. Olympic team, but showed poorly. That bitter disappointment motivated her to work harder for the 1960 Olympics in Rome; and there, Wilma Rudolph won three gold medals! The most a woman had ever won."

Whether they were in business, sports, entertainment, arts, science, politics, or religion, running through the stories of successful people, you will inevitably find the common thread of perseverance, which eventually has led action-oriented champions to success.

Famed composer Beethoven was deaf, yet he did not let this stand in the way of his passion for music. Many of his compositions reveal a strong will to overcome any circumstance. It's as though Beethoven, through his inexplicable calmness and depth in his music, was telling himself, *Accept your flaw, persevere, and know who you are.*

Whether you enjoy his genre of music, it is not difficult to see that Ray Charles was a real-life object lesson of what it means to never quit in spite of being greatly disadvantaged. The twelve-time Grammy Award winner lost his sight when he was six years old, but he had a mother who instilled in him the true extent of his capabilities. She said, "Ray, you've lost your sight, but you haven't lost your mind. You can still create a productive life for yourself." As a young African American boy who was poor, blind, and from the south, Ray could easily have cast himself as a victim. However, as Ray thought about what he really wanted to do with his life, he dreamed of becoming a recording artist.

As a child, Ray Charles would practice playing the piano and singing each day. A teacher heard Ray practicing at school and told him, "Ray, you can't play the piano, and God knows you can't sing. You had better learn how to weave chairs so you can support yourself." This type of comment would stop most people, but it did not deter Ray from his goal. He deeply wanted to become a professional musician and remained focused on his dream.

Many times after auditions, people would tell him that he should just quit, that he couldn't carry a tune in a bucket. But Ray continued. Ultimately Ray's perseverance resulted in his receiving countless awards for his music, which included twelve Grammys. Ray Charles performed before millions of people, including presidents and heads of state. His unique musical style made a lasting imprint on all forms of popular music over the past fifty years.

Ray Charles's prescription for accomplishing his musical dream was simple. He refused to listen to negative people and refused to quit.

Think about a recent task that you thought was insurmountable. In comparison to the challenges faced by the above list of people, was it really that difficult to accomplish? Were the obstacles really that severe? Could an application of perseverance have overcome those impediments? How can you develop the traits of perseverance within yourself that lead you to your ultimate goal?

Here are five simple steps to follow in order to cultivate the trait of perseverance.

Step 1: Continually Focus on the Benefits of Completing the Task

Focusing on the benefits tends to generate the interest, enthusiasm, and passion that provide the energy to accomplish the task.

Austrian-born violinist and composer Fritz Kreisler testified to this point when he said, as quoted in *Guideposts* magazine, "Narrow is the road that leads to the life of a violinist. Hour after hour, day after day and week after week, for years, I lived with my violin. There were so many things that I wanted to do that I had to leave undone; there were so many places I wanted to go that I had to miss if I was to master the violin. The road that I traveled was a narrow road and the way was hard."

Having said that, there was no doubt in Fritz's mind what his priority was. He focused on the benefits that would come to him the day he would be able to master his art. As a result of this, Fritz Kreisler, with his distinctly sweet tone and expressive phrasing, rose to become one of the most famous violinists of his day.

Step 2: Follow Through with the Tasks at Hand No Matter What

Show evidence of purposeful, continuous commitment to all activities, instead of performing sporadic efforts in diverse areas. Those other areas may not be pertinent to completing your goal.

Step 3: Develop a Commitment Not to Abandon Tasks When Faced with an Obstacle

Approach tasks with urgency, tenacity, and doggedness.

Michael A. Guido of Metter, Georgia, a columnist for several newspapers, once wrote, "An artist in Mexico lost his right hand while working on a statue. But he did not give up his work. He learned to carve with his left hand. His beautifully finished masterpiece was called 'In Spite Of.'"

Step 4: Never Stop Believing in Yourself

Believe that you can make things happen by the grace of

God. Think of all the additional talents that you can bring to the completion of the task.

Step 5: Engage Others to Help

Additional strengths, ideas, talent, and skills that others can provide will help get the task completed. In addition, you may learn tricks and techniques that you did not know before.

Step 6: Visualize Your Success

An article in *Soundings* magazine reported the following story: "Liu Chi Kung, who placed second to Van Cliburn in the 1948 Tchaikovsky competition, was imprisoned a year later during the Cultural Revolution in China. During the entire seven years he was held he was denied the use of a piano. Soon after his release, however, he was back on tour. Critics wrote in astonishment that his musicianship was better than ever. 'How did you do this?' a critic asked. 'You had no chance to practice for seven years.'

"'I did practice!' Liu replied. 'Every day I rehearsed every piece I have ever played, note by note, in my mind.'"

History is filled with individuals whose success is attributed to exercising these powerful principles of persistence. One such man you may readily recognize. In fact, most likely you are acquainted with his delight. Colonel Sanders was sixty-five years old when he embarked upon his dream. This came after his former business was forced to close down. Left with an income of only $105 a month in the form of a Social Security check, Colonel Sanders wasn't about to lay down and die. He still had the vibrancy of life within him, and a dream to accomplish great things.

Set Yourself on Fire!

In asking himself this one empowering question, "What can I do that will bring value for other people?" came an answer that would set the course of his dream. Colonel Sanders was an outstanding cook, but he had to get people to know it. His specialty was a wonderful chicken recipe he knew. Equipped with his recipe, he decided to get in his car and drive around to restaurants asking whether they'd buy his recipe. He thought if he would sell it, perhaps he'd get a percentage of their takings. His approach did not succeed, and he only got responses such as, "Why would I want to buy an old man's recipe?"

With each rejection, he would learn from it and change his approach slightly. Continually and doggedly putting forth his best effort, he was passionately convinced that he had a winning recipe. Colonel Sanders had set himself on fire, and nothing was going to stand between him and his dream! For two years, he incessantly drove throughout the United Sates in his old car, knocking on doors attempting to sell his recipe. His persistence paid off. He had visited 1,009 restaurant owners, and all of them turned him down. It wasn't until he knocked on door 1,010 that he succeeded. The rest is history. Today KFC is a household name and is in over eighty countries and territories, with over eleven thousand locations worldwide.

There is no doubt that persistence pays off! They key is to believe in what you are doing and never, never, never quit!

This type of tenacity reminds us of another great man who refused to accept defeat, regardless of the magnitude of the adversity. He knew that persistence was the key to victory. On October 29, 1941, he rose to the occasion, speaking these powerful and immortal words: "Never give in. Never give in. Never, never, never, never—in nothing, great or small, large or petty—never give in, except to convictions of honor and good sense. Never yield to force. Never yield to the apparently overwhelming might of the enemy."

Set Yourself on Fire!

Many historians believe that Churchill's inspiring speeches of faith and persistence made the difference between failure and victory. This persistence rallied Britain and the Allied forces to triumph. Winston Churchill had to set himself on fire, and with it he awoke a nation to believe in itself, and to never give in!

To put it simply, "Winners never quit, and quitters never win." If one is to achieve one's dreams, persistence is an equation to success that in most people can never be omitted. If you are ever faced with the prospect of giving up, you may want to remember these powerful words from the poem, "When Things Go Wrong":

When things go wrong, as they sometimes will,
When the road you're trudging seems all up hill.
When funds are low and the debts are high,
And you want to smile, but you have to sigh.
When care is pressing you down a bit—
Rest, if you must, but don't you quit.
Life is queer with its twists and turns,
As every one of us sometimes learns,
And many a failure turns about
When he might have won had he stuck it out.
Don't give up though the pace seems slow—
You may succeed with another blow.
*   Often the goal is nearer than*
It seems to a faint and faltering man;
Often the struggler has given up
When he might have captured the victor's cup;
And he learned too late when the night came down,
How close he was to the golden crown.
*   Success is failure turned inside out—*
The silver tint of the clouds of doubt,
And you never can tell how close you are,
It may be near when it seems so far:

Set Yourself on Fire!

So stick to the fight when you're hardest hit—
It's when things seem worst that you must not quit.

If there is one secret to success, it is found in the simple, yet powerful quality of persistence. Never, never, never give up!

A Point to Consider

The great aim of education is not knowledge, but action!

Questions to Ponder

1. What knowledge do you have in your possession right now that can be immediately implemented into positive and effective action?
2. What action step will you make today that will propel you toward the achievement of your ultimate goal?

5

FANNING THE FLAME!

"The most powerful weapon on earth is the human soul on fire!"
— Ferdinand Foch

Enthusiasm! Just the mere mention of the word evokes excitement, doesn't it? It is no wonder the legendary playwright Tennessee Williams declared, "Enthusiasm was the most important thing in life!"

When I first came across this quote I quickly dismissed it, while also thinking to myself, *Enthusiasm is one of the most important personal qualities that one can possess. But to say it is the most important is a little bit of a stretch. Isn't it?* Then I began giving further thought to what enthusiasm really means.

The word "enthusiasm" is derived from the ancient Greek word *enthousiasmos*, which contains two words—*en* meaning "in, within," and *Theos*, meaning "God." As I began to consider its deeper meaning, I suddenly realized that Tennessee Williams was right! What can be more empowering than to have in your possession the meaning of "God within"? What wonderful, powerful, and all-encompassing virtue! For with it carries all of whom and what God is, encompassing all of His virtues, including love, joy, peace, goodness, kindness, strength, and power!

In fact, when one really looks deeply into the essence of enthusiasm, one finds all of these virtues.

Set Yourself on Fire!

Enthusiasm Means Love

Have you ever seen two people madly in love with one another? If you have, there is one noticeable expression, and that is enthusiasm. They're excited, they're alive! Being enthusiastic means you're in love—whether it is in love with a person, a job, an endeavor, a purpose, or whatever it may be! One cannot separate enthusiasm from love, or love from enthusiasm. They go hand in hand.

Enthusiasm Means Joy

Have you ever noticed that it is virtually impossible to be enthusiastic without being joyful? Try it! Impossible! Joy is enthusiasm's constant companion.

Enthusiasm Means Peace

As love and joy are interwoven with enthusiasm, another life-enhancing virtue emerges: a sense of deep contentment, a sense of peace. One may not immediately think of associating peace with enthusiasm, but it is definitely there—a peace that says you are living on purpose, on the right track, and what you are doing is true to God, yourself, and others. This authentic experience of inner peace strengthens the inner soul, which then translates itself into an expression of conviction and enthusiasm.

Enthusiasm Means Power

Enthusiasm is a power to execute your dreams in spite of opposition and adversity. It is the very fuel that ignites the engine of your dreams and propels you with the inner power to achieve!

Ferdinand Foch, a French soldier, military theorist, and writer, was credited with possessing "the most original and subtle mind in the French army" in the early twentieth century. Ultimately, he was selected and recognized as the general who led the Allied forces to victory in the First World War. In revealing his secret weapon, he declared, "The most powerful weapon on earth is a human soul on fire!" He knew what it took to win the war, and on the top of the list were men of valor, who burned with enthusiasm for the values that they were defending. Never underestimate the power of enthusiasm!

Enthusiasm Means Hope

Enthusiasm is so comprehensive that it is the very driving force that gives us power, and with this power we obtain hope—a hope that loudly declares, yes, our endeavors can be achieved and it is possible! Have you ever seen a football team down by a few points in the last two minutes of a game? If they could only get to a certain point on the field and kick that winning field goal, or better still throw the ball in the end zone for a touchdown? Then they would win! But what if the team trotted on the field showing no enthusiasm? What would be the chances of them accomplishing the goal? The enthusiasm of the players to win the game brings hope to the team, the coach, and the fans!

Without enthusiasm there is no power, and without power there is no hope. Perhaps this is why Emerson said, "Enthusiasm is the mother of effort, and without it nothing great has ever been achieved."

Set Yourself on Fire!

The Source of Enthusiasm

Just as an apple tree produces apples, an orange tree produces oranges, a raspberry bush produces raspberries, and so on, so the fruit of enthusiasm has its root source in the tree of life we call passion.

Once you are burning with a passion for whatever you do, one thing is for certain: you will flare up with this empowering essence called enthusiasm! The key is to do and to be wonderfully obsessed with what you absolutely love. Do what you love, and the enthusiasm will follow.

There is no question that Martin Luther King Jr. had enthusiasm. It sparkled in his eyes; it vibrated in his voice. Through his passion came forth a spirit of enthusiasm, which made him one of the most notable and influential speakers in American history.

What was his secret? Find the very thing or cause about which you are most passionate. Martin Luther King Jr. hit the nail on the head when he declared, "If a man hasn't found something for which he is willing to die for, he is not fit to live!" What a powerful statement! Now stop and ask yourself: what is in my own life that I'm so passionate about that I would readily lay down my life for its cause? Whatever the answer is to that question, that's exactly where your heart is, and from that heart springs forth the well of life and the fire of enthusiasm.

Best-selling author and speaker Jack Canfield once said, "One of the things that may get in the way of people being lifelong learners is that they're not in touch with their passion. If you're passionate about what it is you do, then you're going to be looking for everything you can to get better at it."

In this life we are all given a certain amount of time to define who we are, our beliefs, our purpose, and how we will live our lives. The clock is ticking. Isn't life too short to be living any other way than to set yourself on fire with passion?

Here is a question to consider: are you living or simply existing? Living passionately is moving from the safe confines of mere existence to purposeful living!

Do you want to go through life not failing? Here's the secret: "Never try!" Never try anything of significance or meaning.

The Psalmist David certainly had passion when he wrote, "As a deer pants for streams of water so my soul pants for you, O God!" (Psalm 42:1), thus expressing his heart's palpitating desire to know God.

Some people in life seek to extinguish your flame by pouring on the water of negativity, by criticizing, by doing whatever they can to rain on your parade. Don't let them! Nobody can make you feel inferior or bad about yourself unless you let them.

You choose every day what kind of day it's going to be—nobody else.

Author Deepak Chopra summarized it well when he stated, "To have passion, to have a dream, to have a purpose in life. And there are three components to that purpose. One is to find out who you really are, to discover God. The second is to serve other human beings, because we are here to do that. And the third is to express your unique talents, and when you are expressing your unique talents you lose track of time."

What to Do If Your Flame Begins to Flutter

There is no doubt that enthusiasm is the power that energizes you toward your dreams, gives you the strength to overcome even the greatest of challenges, and gives reason for your life. But what if, somehow, somewhere along the way, your flame starts to wither? Has that ever happened to you? Have you ever started off with great excitement and enthusiasm, and somehow, somewhere, it gets dampened by life's challenges?

Here are seven ways in which you can fan the flame back into a blazing fire!

1. Fill Your Mind with Positive Books and Audio Programs

Every now and then I'll have someone come up to me and say, "Ah, all that positive, motivational stuff doesn't last!"

Well, my reply to that is simple. "A shower doesn't either, but it's a good thing to take one once in a while!" You see, a good bath or shower is not supposed to last you the whole week. In fact, it's highly recommended that one should take one every day to keep smelling fresh and clean. And so it is with motivation. Motivation is not something we need to take only once in a while, whenever it's convenient. It's an essential. A good shower may last for a day, and in the same way so does soaking in positive, life-enhancing thoughts that clean our minds and attitudes from the dirt that we can be exposed to on a daily basis. Keeping an enthusiastic attitude depends highly on the thoughts we choose to let into our minds, so it is essential to do this on a constant level to maintain that high level of enthusiasm.

2. Stick with the Winners

The late and great Charlie "Tremendous" Jones was famous for saying, "You are today what you'll be five years from now except for two things, the people you meet and the books you read." No doubt, Charlie was the epitome of enthusiasm. When I talked with him or heard his voice, I would get excited. He lived his message, and his enthusiasm was contagious.

Stay close to those who inspire you, and who make you feel good and happy. And if I may suggest, stay far away from the gripers, complainers, and gossips—those who have little to nothing good to say about anything. You will become like the people you choose to surround yourself with. Want to be a bright, positive influence on others? Hang around bright, positive people! Want to be miserable and complaining? Hang around miserable and negative people. It's as simple as that.

3. Count Your Blessings

I'm often asked, particularly after speaking engagements when I've shared some of my triumphs over adversity, "How did you do it? How did you pull yourself from that dark place?" The answer is basically simple. It's found in this empowering word: "gratitude." There was a time in my life when I thought things were going pretty bad. I kept focusing on how bad things were and what I didn't have, and that would just sink me into a lower state of mind.

Then one day a friend gave me some pretty good advice. He said, "Phil, instead of thinking on those things that aren't going right for you, why don't you, when you wake up in the morning, count out those seven things you are grateful for most?" Well, figuring that I didn't have much to lose from taking his advice, I began doing just that.

Today, first thing in the morning I find myself charged up for each day by counting out the seven things for which I'm most grateful. And guess what? It works! Big time! Often when I wake up, the first thing I do is give thanks for the fact that I'm alive. I go to the window to pull back the drapes; often see a bright, beautiful day; hear the chirping of the birds; see the bright sunshine; and give thanks that I live in such a beautiful country, where I can be free! I hop and skip to the kitchen table, and grab my box of Froot Loops and a pint of milk. And as I begin pouring my breakfast, it dawns on me that I'm one of the privileged few in a world that goes hungry who has the luxury of eating three meals a day. I ponder the thought with a deep sense of somber gratitude, and then I see my three lovely cats! They are always so close whenever I'm eating a meal, and I pick them up, hug them, and kiss them all over as they make me smile and laugh. And my heart swells up with a sense of joy and excitement that I have them in my life. By this time, I'm only halfway through my gratitude count on point four or five. I'm already feeling totally charged up. By the time I finish my gratitude count, which follows me right into the shower and out again, I'm so excited I'm just about to fly out of the house!

What do you have to be grateful for? Can you identify at least seven things for which you can give thanks? Take a moment or two right now and try it. See how it makes you smile, laugh, and feel good.

It's been said, "Gratitude is born in the heart of those who take the time to count their blessings." Now that's enthusiasm!

4. See the Joy and Humor in Life

Don't know if you've noticed, but life really is full of humor. Humor can be seen everywhere, in nature, in animals, in people, and most of all in us! Learn to see the humor in adversity; in fact that is probably where you'll find most of it. It's all in how we see things. Most of us take things way too seriously.

If ever we lose our enthusiasm, it is often because we fail to see the humor in life. The Bible points out that a merry heart is like medicine to the soul. Even in the most trying circumstances, we can find the healing and revitalizing essence of merriment or laughter.

In *The Anatomy of an Illness: As Perceived by the Patient*, Norman Cousins tells of being hospitalized with a rare, crippling disease. When he was diagnosed as incurable, Cousins checked out of the hospital. Aware of the harmful effects negative emotions can have on the body, Cousins reasoned the reverse was true. So he borrowed a movie projector and prescribed his own treatment, consisting of Marx Brothers films and old *Candid Camera* reruns. It didn't take long for him to discover that ten minutes of laughter provided two hours of pain-free sleep. Amazingly, his debilitating disease was eventually reversed. After the account of his victory appeared in the *New England Journal of Medicine*, Cousins received more than three thousand letters from appreciative physicians throughout the world.

When we tap into humor, we begin to feel good, and when we begin to feel good, joy and enthusiasm are not too far away.

5. Play Your Favorite Music; Dance Like Nobody's Watching

Probably the quickest and most energizing way to evoke enthusiasm is to fill your senses with music. I know one speaker who, before he hits the platform to speak, puts on his iPod and listens to his favorite music. This gets his enthusiasm up. He hits the stage and is able to perform at his best. Years ago when I started my sales career in residential sales, I spent a few minutes in the car listening to my favorite songs. This put me into a positive mind-set, and more often than not, I'd walk away with the sale. Often I'll just put on my favorite music, pick up my cats, and start dancing with them! We have a great time together, and this also keeps my enthusiasm going. Music and dancing are powerful methods for helping spur and maintain your enthusiasm.

6. Spend Time in Meditation

We've touched on numerous ways in which you can awaken your enthusiasm. However, as odd as this may seem, probably the most profound way I've found to draw out true and lasting enthusiasm is to spend time in prayer and meditation. This is where and when I quiet my heart and tap into the source of enthusiasm itself—God! We all have the means to do this. There is no doubt in my heart that there is a beautiful, loving, supreme being who is the creator of the universe. When I approach the God of the universe and come to Him, laying out my heart, my thoughts, and my prayers, I consequently have taken the time in the quietness of my own heart to hear that still small voice from within. Often, even after I have wept, I'm awakened to a new sense of vigor, a peace, and a renewed sense of joy that compel within me an *enthousiasmos* (God within)! What can be more exciting and empowering than a sense that you are at one with the creator of heaven and earth, and to experience a deep, genuine experience with the almighty God, who bestows untold joy and blessings upon us all? I often awaken from this experience with a sense of great joy and singing in my heart. God is love, power, and the very source of enthusiasm.

7. Act Enthusiastic and You'll Be Enthusiastic

Funny, but true! Enthusiasm is often only a question of how we maintain our body posture. Just for a moment, act as if you have won a $10 million prize or a new car, or have purchased your dream home, or fallen wonderfully in love with the person of your dreams. Just take a moment. How would you express yourself? Just the acting out of enthusiasm will bring on enthusiasm. Exercise enthusiasm in your speech, in your everyday conduct, no matter how you feel, and within seconds you'll find yourself expressing enthusiasm. It's fun! Try it!

The Bottom Line

Find something worthwhile that you truly believe in; find what you are most passionate about. Make it the center of all your thoughts and activities, and enthusiasm will erupt from within like a volcano, spilling out in everything you say and do.

Famed English professor and novelist Charles Kingsley couldn't have put it in better terms when he stated, "We act as though comfort and luxury were the chief requirements of life, when all that we need to make us happy is something to be enthusiastic about."

That's the bottom line. That's what living with joy and passion is all about. So here's the loaded question. What are you most passionate about? If there were no such thing as money, what would you be doing with your life? Whatever the answer to that question is, may I suggest that the answer might be exactly what you should be doing. Follow your heart and follow your dream, what innately burns within you as an expression of your life's purpose, and you will find that empowering, life-propelling virtue we call enthusiasm!

A Point to Consider

The word "enthusiasm" is derived from the ancient Greek word *enthousiasmos*, which comprises two words:

en, meaning "in, within," and *Theos*, meaning "God." What can possibly be more empowering than to carry within your heart the expression of the word that means "God within?"

Questions to Ponder

1. What seven things can I count out right now for which I am most grateful?
2. What am I most passionate about?

6

THE GIFT OF ADVERSITY

"Adversity collapses around a true adherent soul."
—Jareb Teague

Have you ever wondered why we must face so much adversity in life?

A man found a cocoon of a butterfly. One day a small opening appeared; he sat and watched the butterfly for several hours as it struggled to force its body through that little hole. Then it seemed to stop making any progress. It appeared as if it had gotten as far as it could and it could go no further.

Then the man decided to help the butterfly, so he took a pair of scissors and snipped off the remaining bit of the cocoon. The butterfly then emerged easily. But it had a swollen body and small, shriveled wings. The man continued to watch the butterfly because he expected that, at any moment, the wings would enlarge and expand to be able to support the body, which would contract in time.

Neither happened! In fact, the butterfly spent the rest of its life crawling around with a swollen body and shriveled wings. It never was able to fly.

What the man in his kindness and haste did not understand was that the restricting cocoon and the struggle are requirements for the butterfly's growth. Going through the tiny opening were nature's way of forcing fluid from the body of the butterfly into its wings, so that it would be ready for flight once it achieved its freedom from the cocoon.

Sometimes struggles are exactly what we need in our life.

Set Yourself on Fire!

If nature allowed us to go through our life without any obstacles, it would cripple us. We would not be as strong as what we could have been. And we could never fly!

If there ever was one outstanding, common denominator that ties all great achievers together, all of them, every one of them, had to overcome enormous adversity of some type or another before they finally met up with success. I've never met, known, or read about anyone who has achieved success—whether it was in the arena of science, the arts, business, politics, or any other venue for that matter—who didn't have to endure and overcome adversity. As we study the lives of those who made significant contributions in our world (as we did in chapter 1), we find that they all faced great challenges at some point or another along their journey.

It is as if nature had set it up in such a way that overcoming adversity would be the very price of admission required to achieve their destiny.

As I have observed adversity in my own life, I'm convinced that adversity comes not as a curse but as an act of a loving, benevolent God, who wishes to teach us something vital that will help us adjust the course of our direction at times, and to make us more loving, wiser, and stronger.

King Solomon brought insight to this understanding when he wrote, "Do not reject the discipline of the Lord or loathe His reproof, for whom the Lord loves He reproves, even as a father corrects the son in whom He delights" (Proverbs 3:11–12).

Mother Theresa once said, "I know that God won't give me anything I can't handle. I just wish He didn't trust me so much."

The truth of the matter is there are so many jewels of insight, hidden gifts of strength and wisdom that are designed in preparing us to fulfill our ultimate purpose.

Set Yourself on Fire!

The Purposes of Adversity

There are three main purposes of adversity.

The First Purpose Is to Test Us and Help Define Who We Are

The following story comes from clarkeching.com:

A young woman went to her mother and told her about her life and how things were so hard for her. She did not know how she was going to make it and wanted to give up. She was tired of fighting and struggling. It seemed as one problem was solved, a new one arose.

Her mother took her to the kitchen. She filled three pots with water and placed each on a high fire. Soon the pots came to boil. In the first she placed carrots, in the second she placed eggs, and in the last she placed ground coffee beans. She let them sit and boil, without saying a word.

In about twenty minutes she turned off the burners. She fished the carrots out and placed them in a bowl. She pulled the eggs out and placed them in a bowl. Then she ladled the coffee out and placed it in a bowl.

Turning to her daughter, she asked, "Tell me what you see."

"Carrots, eggs, and coffee," her daughter replied.

Her mother brought her closer and asked her to feel the carrots. She did and noted that they were soft. The mother then asked the daughter to take an egg and break it. After pulling off the shell, she observed the hard-boiled egg. Finally, the mother asked the daughter to sip the coffee. The daughter smiled. As she smelled its rich aroma, the daughter then asked, "What does it mean, Mother?"

Her mother explained that each of these objects had faced the same adversity: boiling water. Each reacted differently. The carrot went in strong, hard, and unrelenting. However, after being subjected to the boiling water, it softened and became weak. The egg had been fragile. Its thin outer shell had protected its liquid interior, but after sitting through the boiling water, its inside became hardened. The ground coffee beans were unique, however. After they were in the boiling water, they had   changed the water.

"Which are you?" she asked her daughter.

"When adversity knocks on your door, how do you respond? Are you a carrot, an egg or a coffee bean?

"Think of this: Which am I? Am I the carrot that seems strong, but with pain and adversity do I wilt and become soft and lose my strength?

"Am I the egg that starts with a malleable heart, but changes with the heat? Did I have a fluid spirit, but after a death, a breakup, a financial hardship or some other trial, have I become hardened and stiff? Does my shell look the same, but on the inside am I bitter and tough with a stiff spirit and hardened heart?

"Or am I like the coffee bean? The bean actually changes the hot water, the very circumstance that brings the pain. When the water gets hot, it releases the fragrance and flavor. If you are like the bean, when things are at their worst, you get better and change the situation around you. When the hour is the darkest and trials are their greatest, do you elevate yourself to another level? How do you handle adversity? Are you a carrot, an egg or a coffee bean?"

May you have enough happiness to make you sweet, enough trials to make you strong, enough sorrow to keep you human, and enough hope to make you happy.

The happiest of people don't necessarily have the best of everything; they just make the most of everything that comes along their way. The brightest future will always be based on a forgotten past; you can't go forward in life until you let go of your past failures and heartaches.

Robert Schuller summed it up well when he stated, "The adversity we face in life will either make us a bitter person or a better person. The choice is ours."

The Second Purpose Is to Teach Us a Wide Array of Important Insights

Famous British author and journalist Malcolm Muggeridge noted, "Contrary to what might be expected, I look back on experiences that at the time seemed especially desolating and painful with particular satisfaction. Indeed, I can say with complete truthfulness that everything I have learned in my seventy-five years in this world, everything that has truly enhanced and enlightened my experience, has been through affliction."

Adversity can teach us how certain approaches don't work.

Thomas Edison certainly knew the value in adversity and in what many people might have seen as failure. It is said that Thomas Edison performed fifty thousand experiments before he succeeded in producing a storage battery. We might assume the famous inventor would have had some serious doubts along the way. But when asked if he ever became discouraged working so long without results, Edison replied, "Results? Why, I know fifty thousand things that won't work."

Set Yourself on Fire!

In learning and building on his lessons of failure, Edison was able to draw closer to the solution, until he finally achieved the desired result.

Adversity can teach us certain values and virtues.

As a young boy, I grew up in somewhat of a confused state of affairs. I did not understand situations that were going on around and about me. Beliefs were imposed upon me, authority was abusive, and certain things that people said and did just didn't seem to add up with what they claimed to believe or be. As an impressionable young boy, this was deeply confusing, hurtful, and disheartening. *What was the truth?* I would often ask myself.

Then one day, when I was fourteen years old, a day I will never forget, I remember reading a proverb that had a profound effect on me and forever forged my approach to life. It stated, "Do not let kindness and truth leave you, bind them around your neck, write them on the tablet of your heart, so you will find favor and good repute in the sight of God and man" (Proverbs 3:3–4).

Somehow, these words resonated deeply within my soul. "Kindness and truth" seemed to make all the sense in the world to me. Kindness: If a person claimed to be a person possessing truth, and yet did not exemplify simple kindness, their truth didn't and doesn't in my viewpoint amount to much, if anything. Simple kindness was and is the manifestation that one has love. It affirms in a large way that a person possesses the second principle, which is Truth. After all, what did Saint Paul write when he stated, "love is kind"? He went on to affirm in the letter to the Corinthians that if you have all knowledge, and do not have this kind of love it avails to nothing. So what was he saying? An absence of love in one's life wipes out the value of any knowledge and truth that one may proclaim to have.

If you want to see if someone possesses the mark of what truth is, see if they possess the attribute of love, and at the very least, one of its by-products, which is the expression of kindness. The apostle John noted and exhorted his readers, "To love one another, for love is from God; and everyone who loves is born of God and knows God. The one, who does not love, does not know God, for God is love!" (1 John 4:7–8).

I was raised the son of a preacher, immersed in religious settings all of my young life, and went on to study theology in college, only to get kicked out in my second year. It still amazes me that there are many people, particularly many leaders (bless their hearts) within religious circles, who don't seem to understand this love and truth. My conclusion from these myriad of experiences, and comparing them to what Jesus spoke about, is that I realize that what they are saying cannot be the complete truth, because all truth is embedded in the expression of love, a love that at the very least expresses simple kindness.

After all, the Bible says, "Speak the truth in love" (Ephesians 4:15).

Moreover, from a practical standpoint, there is a saying, "People don't care how much you know, until they know how much you care."

A great communicator or an effective leader is one who genuinely puts a sincere attitude of care, kindness, and truthfulness in the center of his heart. It is no wonder that King Solomon, who stated these principles millennia ago, said that the one who does this would be a great influencer, an individual who ultimately finds favor in the sight of God and man.

Moreover, I discovered that in asking for the virtues of kindness and truth at a young age, I was given a revelation and a thirst for it in the most peculiar way. Where I thought God would lavish me with a surrounding of experiences that would clearly exemplify kindness and truth, I was exposed from that point on to what I can deem as only an unusual amount of cruelty and unfairness throughout my life.

This is not what I expected. After all, did I not pray for kindness and truth? But I have discovered gifts from God sometimes do not come in the shape and form we expect them. Often they come in insurmountably wise and clever disguises. In being exposed to unkindness I found the meaning of what kindness is and is not. In being exposed to deceit, I understood the meaning of what integrity is and is not.

Without these experiences of adversity, I do believe I would not have the understanding that has been granted to me.

I suppose it is very much like the paradox that light cannot be fully appreciated and understood until one has experienced darkness. One does not fully appreciate and understand the essence of freedom until experiencing imprisonment, and one might not fully appreciate the value of good health until experiencing poor health. Life is filled with these incredible paradoxes of insight.

In the final analysis, I look back and delight in my difficulties, for they have been my teachers, and have been the very motivation that spurs me forward in the pursuit of these two life-enhancing principles.

The Third Purpose Is That Adversity Will Introduce Us to an Underdeveloped Part of Mental and Physical Potential

In 1977, a sixty-three-year-old woman by the name of Laura Schultz was in the house when suddenly she heard a scream. The car that her grandson was working on had collapsed on his arm. In a quick, desperate reaction, it was reported that she ran out and somehow helped to lift the car just enough for her grandson to get out from under it—an exceptional task, considering she had never lifted anything heavier than a fifty-pound bag of cat food before that incident. Often it is never until a real crisis sets in or until we are faced with a great challenge that we ever get introduced to our "other and greater selves," thus discovering what we are truly capable of doing.

What is particularly interesting about this story is that Laura Schultz had initially refused to talk about the incident. The reason, she later admitted in an interview, was because it challenged her beliefs about what could and could not be done. If she was able to do this when she thought she couldn't, "What does that say about the rest of my life?" she rationalized.

As a result of being encouraged and helped by Dr. Charles Garfield, the very man who came to interview her, Laura broke through her self-imposed thought barriers to pursue her dream. That incident of adversity woke her up to the understanding of infinite possibilities!

Napoleon Hill observed, after conducting over six hundred interviews with some of the most successful people in his era, that those who overcame their obstacles were those who were able to put their struggles and adversity into their proper light.

He noted that with every failure came an equal seed of opportunity. What some might consider a curse, others would see as a blessing.

As has been said so many times, "It is not what happens to you that matters, but what you do with what happens to you that matters."

No one seemed to know this better than W. Mitchell, who at the age of twenty-eight survived a terrible motorcycle crash, which resulted in third-degree burns covering three-quarters of his body. Moreover, the accident burned his face beyond recognition, and also resulted in having all his fingers and thumbs amputated. This left him with two stumps where his hands used to be.

Although there appeared little hope that W. Mitchell would

live, miraculously he survived after extensive operations, which included sixteen skin grafts and thirteen transfusions.

While he lay for weeks in the hospital bed, he found inner strength through an internal conviction that he must have survived for a purpose, and that his life was not over.

This by all means was not the end for W. Mitchell. With a remarkable thirst for life and a determination that he would not allow this accident to deter him from living the life of his dreams, he was back on his feet again within six months.

He cofounded a tiny company in Vermont, which quickly grew to become the second largest employer in the state. His courage, hard work, and perseverance had paid off and earned him a financial net worth that was in the millions.

He purchased a beautiful home and an airplane. Soon after, he was up to even bigger challenges as he decided to run for mayor, and he won. He also ran for Congress, and although his face was grotesquely disfigured by the bike accident, he turned his scars into stars with a champion campaign slogan that declared, "Send me to Congress, and I won't be just another pretty face!"

Regardless of his earlier encounter with adversity and his many triumphs in between, adversity was still not finished with W. Mitchell.

On November 11, 1975, the personal plane that he was piloting encountered unfavorable weather conditions and consequently crashed. Once again W. Mitchell miraculously survived, but the accident crushed his spinal cord and left him without the use of his legs. Now, not only did he have to contend with the permanent burns and a disfigured body, but he would not be able to ever use his legs again.

Did that keep W. Mitchell down? Not a chance! What was W. Mitchell's attitude? Instead of focusing on what he no longer was able to do because of his injuries, he focused on what he still could do. Whenever asked how he would deal with life and his set of adversities, his response was always this: "Before my accidents, there were ten thousand things I could do. I could either spend the rest of my life dwelling on the one thousand that I had lost, or instead choose to focus on the nine thousand I still had left."

Today W. Mitchell travels the world as a motivational speaker, inspiring thousands by sharing his empowering message of hope and courage in overcoming adversity.

Although he needs a wheelchair and cannot walk, by no means does a wheelchair confine him. He enjoys living life to the fullest. Among his many recreational activities, he enjoys whitewater rafting and he skydives! Imagine that!

If that isn't enough, he sits on numerous boards as an enormously successful businessman, having cofounded another company, and he has also has become the chair of a $65 million company!

W. Mitchell never lost sight of the fact that regardless of what happened to him, there was a purpose for it, and no matter what, he always had a choice: to let life's circumstances make him a bitter person or a better person. The choice is ours.

If there is one certainty about life, it is that adversity will strike whether we like it or not. It's all part of living. As the age-old proverb states, "The rain will fall on the just and the unjust" (Matthew 5:45). So it is not a matter of whether it will come, but what do we do and how do we respond to it when it does.

Failure is never final, but it brings important stepping-stones toward our dreams. We need only to recognize them and embrace the lessons.

The one who has set himself on fire never sees obstacles as obstacles, but sees important, life-empowering principles.

There are three empowering principles to keep in mind when faced with adversity.

Set Yourself on Fire!

Empowering Principle Number One: The person who is set on fire by one's dream never sees failure as failure, but sees failure only as a learning experience.

Thomas Edison certainly knew the great value of adversity or what many observers called failure during his attempt to invent the incandescent lightbulb. In his attempt to do so, it was reported that he "failed" over ten thousand times. Finally, a skeptical reporter came up to him one day and said, "Mr. Edison, how does it feel to have tried and failed ten thousand times?" Edison in his wisdom replied, "I did not fail ten thousand times. I just found ten thousand ways in which it doesn't work!" Where most people saw failure, he saw his failure as success.

In learning and building on his lessons of failure, Edison was able to draw closer to the solution, until he finally achieved success.

Empowering Principle Number Two: The person who sets oneself on fire with a dream never sees failure as failure, but sees it as the necessary information needed to adjust the course of one's direction.

It has been said that insanity is doing the same thing over and over again and expecting a different result. This is why learning from our experiences and adjusting our approach is an essential part of progress and ultimate achievement.

Most of us are familiar with the modern-day torpedo. The modern-day torpedo has a sonar device in its cone. When it is fired from the submarine toward the target, it zigzags and then zeros in. It will start off in the water, and because of the currents, it gets off course. Then the sonar device kicks in and gives a negative indicator that it's off its target and then readjusts.

It readjusts again and focuses on its target. Once again it

sways from its course, the indicator kicks in again, and places it on the right course. This will go on and on during its course until finally it hits the target. The fact is, the majority of the time the torpedo is off target, but it keeps readjusting from the negative feedback until it reaches its goal.

Could you imagine if the torpedo took it personally and went back home? Of course not. The torpedo is systematic in its approach and uses the negative feedback it needs to keep on target. And so it is with the goal achiever, who does not take rejection personally, but uses negative feedback in a constructive way to readjust and keep on course with the target, until reaching the desired result.

Empowering Principle Number Three: The person who sets oneself on fire with a dream never sees failure as failure, but only as an experience to develop a sense of humor.

The joy of living our dreams is not so much in the destination as it is in the journey. Life is to be enjoyed! I have a philosophy about life: "If it's not fun, it's not worth it!" So many of us take ourselves too seriously. A great deal of the fun is seeing the humor in our difficulties and setbacks.

How many of us have ever had a traumatic experience that has wiped us out? We were down, and then months or even years later, we look back and can't stop laughing at the situation. Has that ever happened to you? It sure has to me. You may have noticed that most humorous stories, presentations, and speeches are derived from supposed misfortunes that in looking back on them are not so misfortunate after all.

Laughter is the very antidote that emotionally lifts the pain found in the moment of adversity. King Solomon wrote that "a cheerful heart is good medicine, but a crushed spirit dries up the bones" (Proverbs 17:22). The key is to laugh sooner!

Set Yourself on Fire!

As Robert Schuller put it, "Tough times never last, but tough people do!" No matter how gloomy things may appear, those clouds of darkness eventually break and sunshine reappears.

The key is to keep a positive attitude on life, its circumstances, and challenges no matter what! All the great people I've met seem to delight in seeing the reality of the world and seeing the humor in it. After you have done all you can to make it work, and for some reason it doesn't, take the time to see the humor in it all. Laugh, love, and live! Your sense of humor is what will keep you going through adverse times.

Finally, if you ever feel overwhelmed by your difficulties, it may be helpful to remember the biographical profile of this remarkable individual.

The introduction to his journey began when he was born in the lonely room of a log cabin in Kentucky. He had only a total of eighteen months of formal education, and then faced a great amount of ridicule, and an exhaustive series of defeats, ailments, and seemingly insurmountable challenges throughout his life. This man finally discovered that his adversity was part of the preparation process needed to undertake one of the greatest callings in American history.

- In 1816, at the tender age of seven years old, he had to support his family after they were forced out of their home.
- In 1818, at the age of nine, his mother died.
- In 1831, he failed in business.
- In 1832, he was defeated for the legislature, he lost his job, and couldn't get into law school.
- In 1833, he declared bankruptcy, and spent the next seventeen years of his life paying off the money.

- In 1834, he was defeated for the legislature again.
- In 1835, he was engaged to be married, but his sweetheart died and his heart was broken.
- In 1836, he had a nervous breakdown and spent the next six months in bed.
- In 1838, he was defeated in becoming the speaker in the state legislature.
- In 1840, he was defeated in becoming elector.
- In 1843, he was defeated for Congress.
- In 1846, he was defeated for Congress.
- In 1860, Abraham Lincoln was elected as the sixteenth president of the United States.

The fact of the matter is, as difficult as it may seem at the time, adversity carries with it an equal seed of opportunity. It is a gift from the universe that is preparing you for the ultimate achievement of your life's purpose.

See adversity for what it is—a gift of knowledge, insight, and strength. Not a misfortune, but rather a set of circumstances that is filled with an opportunity for personal growth, a true blessing in disguise!

A Point to Consider

Adversity is a gift in disguise.

Questions to Ponder

1. What benefits have I derived from my adversity?
2. How has my adversity prepared me for a higher purpose?

7

THE WORKSHOP OF THE MIND

Dreaming is where it all begins. No person has achieved anything of any significance until first acquiring it in the form of a thought. The innovators, the leaders, and the achievers of this world are and were great dreamers. As we read in chapter 1, they first saw what they wanted to achieve in their own mind's eye, and coupled with an unwavering faith began to pursue their dream until it became a reality.

No one has ever achieved anything of any significance without the working of this great faculty of the mind called imagination.

George Bernard Shaw put it succinctly when he stated, "Some people see things and say, 'Why?' But I dream things that never were; and say, 'Why not?'"

Imagination is the ability to go beyond the boundaries of the immediate and visualize possibilities that the naked eye cannot see. Imagination anticipates what is to be and acts on it.

Hockey Hall of Famer Wayne Gretzky was one of the most successful players of all time, not only because of his enormous skill, but also because he implemented the use of imagination in his every play. When asked to share his secret of success with an inquiring reporter, Gretzky replied, "I don't go where the puck is, I go where it will be."

Microsoft founders Bill Gates and Paul Allen certainly had imagination well before anyone could visualize the advent of the personal computer and the Internet. While IBM giant failed to see the opportunity for the oncoming tidal wave of demand for personal computers, Gates and Allen clearly visualized a world where there would be a personal computer on every desk. Capitalizing on this dream, Microsoft launched its operating system, which forever changed the world, and of course made them billionaires in the process!

The stories are endless, whether in business, the arts, science, entertainment, or sports. The ones who accomplished the remarkable are the leaders, the innovators, the great ones; they were all individuals who had the capacity to put to use the faculty of the mind that we call the imagination.

Unfortunately, many fail to use this great resource of the mind. Many are like the Iowa farmer of the 1860s who left his field for an hour to watch the construction of the transcontinental railroad near his farm. He watched the track being laid. A few minutes later a steam locomotive came through. The farmer went back to his fields and thought, *So that's what a railroad is all about, tracks and train.* What the farmer failed to see was what was beyond the obvious and the great possibilities that came with the railroad. He didn't see how he could get his products to many new markets, quicker and more efficiently than at the moment. He didn't anticipate the booming of metropolises such as Chicago, Kansas City, Denver, and San Francisco, and the development of intercontinental trade. He didn't see how it would be possible to transport his products across the country in less than a week, and therefore extend his profitability. All he saw were trains and tracks and nothing more, and because of his sight he remained within the boundaries of his self-imposed limitations.

And yet, unlike the farmer from Iowa, there were those, and are those, who can see the forest beyond the trees—who see the diamond in the rough and the opportunities in every situation.

One such individual was the son of a German butcher who immigrated to America as a young man. Coming from humble beginnings, he saw unborn opportunities everywhere. After capitalizing on his dreams and becoming very successful in his own right, John Jacob Astor envisioned even an greater opportunity. In the 1830s he foresaw that the next big boom would be the building up of New York, which would soon emerge as one of the world's greatest cities. Astor withdrew from all his other ventures and used the money to buy and develop large tracts of Manhattan real estate. Predicting and envisioning the rapid growth northward on Manhattan Island, Astor purchased more and more land beyond the city limits of the time. Using more of his imagination, Astor rarely built on his land; instead he let others pay rent to use it.

Although it would be easy for many people in retrospect to say, "Manhattan real estate? That's easy, it takes no genius to figure that one out."

Astor, however, used his active imagination to capitalize on what others failed to see at the time. Toward the end of his life, Astor is quoted as saying, "If I were to live my life all over again, I would buy every square inch of Manhattan." Well, he didn't have to live his life all over again; he fared pretty well to say the least, making him the fourth wealthiest man in American history.

Today there are hundreds of individuals who have put their imagination to use in predicting the untapped potential of the Internet, making common individuals into instant millionaires and even billionaires because of the use of their imagination.

One such individual is Mark Zuckerberg, who while still a college student consumed with his passion for computers began toying around with an invention that is universally known today as Facebook. In February 2004 from his college dorm room, Facebook was launched. What was initially intended as a tool for communication within his own sphere of contacts, inside his school, it quickly spread to other schools within a few short months, and before long hundreds of thousands of people were using Facebook.

Does imagination pays off? In 2009, just a few short years after the launch of his dream, which was born out of his college dorm, Mark, at age twenty-five, was ranked by *Forbes* magazine as the 158th richest person in the United States, with a net worth of $2 billion.

What's more, Mark Zuckerberg and his college buddy Dustin Moskovitz did it by doing what they were most passionate about, and by letting the faculty of their imaginations run free. One could say they had set themselves on fire!

These stories and so many more only come to validate what Albert Einstein meant when he stated, "Imagination is the preview of life's coming attractions."

Imagination Has Always Been a Preview of Life's Coming Attractions

At a time when it was an "established fact" that the earth was the center of the universe, Galileo, in spite of great opposition, dared to challenge this "fact" and imagined different possibilities. His imagination led him to discoveries that today can very well credit him with being the individual most responsible for giving birth to modern science.

At a time when the general consensus was that "the world is flat," Christopher Columbus only had his mind fixed on the opportunity to pursue his dream. He imagined discovering new lands, regardless of the warnings that he would fall off the edge of the earth. He confidently pursued his dream, and the rest is history.

At a time when editorials around the continent, such as one in an 1865 edition of the *Boston Globe*, read, "Well informed people know it is impossible to transmit the voice over wires and even if it were possible to do so, the thing would be of no practical value," Alexander Graham Bell imagined a device that could and would! On March 10, 1867, Bell sent the first message over the telephone to Thomas A. Watson, who assisted him in his workshop. Because of Alexander Graham Bell's extraordinary vision and imagination, the telephone and much of the modern communications we rely on today were invented as a result of what went on in his mind years before the manifestation took place.

At a time when most people held the belief conveyed by British mathematician and physicist Lord Kelvin, which stated, "Heavier-than-air flying machines are impossible," Orville and Wilbur Wright imagined inventing a flying machine that would one day soar the skies. Although they had to endure a lot of ridicule along the way, they held on to the picture they had fixed in their imagination. And today, we can fly from Tokyo to Seattle at such a speed that if we left Tokyo on a Wednesday and someone asked us, "When would we arrive in Seattle?" Because of the change in time and the speed of aerodynamic technology, we could say, "We could arrive yesterday."

At a time when many in the industry overlooked the explosive potential of television, reflecting the words of Darryl F. Zanuck, head honcho of 20th Century Fox, who stated, "Television won't be able to hold any market it captures after the first month. People will soon get tired of starring at a plywood box every night," David Sarnoff (head of RCA) imagined a powerful medium that would and could reach the masses. By the time he translated his ideas into reality, Sarnoff founded the National Broadcasting Company (NBC) and led the ever-growing telecommunications and consumer electronics company into becoming one of the largest companies in the world.

At a time when it was called "the impossible dream," so-called experts such as astronomer Dr. Forest Ray Moulton of the University of Chicago echoed the thinking of most people of his time. He stated, "There is no hope for the fanciful idea of reaching the Moon because of insurmountable barriers in escaping the Earth's gravity." Yet on July 20, 1969, the seemingly impossible was achieved, as the childhood dream that lay within the imagination of Neil Armstrong became a reality, as he became the first person to ever step on the moon.

And of course, how can we leave out this one? Because of oversights by so many "experts" in the computer industry, which could be summed up in the words of former president Ken Olson of Digital Corporation, who concluded, "There is no reason for any individual to have a computer in their home," Bill Gates imagined the very opposite, a world where every individual would have a very good reason to have a computer in their home. And today we are still only seeing the tip of this massive information technology industry, with no end in sight.

In life, as you pursue your dream and what is most meaningful to you, you'll always meet up with plenty of naysayers who will say, "It can't be done!"

The important thing, and the only thing that really matters, is that you never stop believing for yourself, "It can be done!"

As Henry Ford said, "If you think you can, or you think you can't, you're right."

At the end of the day the only thing that really matters is whether you think you can or not. Limitations are only the barriers we set in our own minds. If we use our imagination, the possibilities are boundless!

Extensive research in the field of human development has unveiled time and time again that we are only tapping into a very small percentage of our mental and physical resources. At best most individuals use up to only 10 percent of the resources available to them.

Set Yourself on Fire!

William James foreshadowed this discovery when he stated, "Compared to what we ought to be, we are only half awake. We are making use of only a small part of our mental and physical resources."

Tapping into the Resources of Our Mind

If this is the case, and researchers say it is, the question now becomes, "What is standing in the way of tapping into the rich resources of the mind, and how can we begin to truly excavate our innate creativity?"

The fact is that we all have extraordinary capabilities to use the facet of our imagination. As humans we have a built-in creative mechanism, and our ability to tap into this mechanism can and will make a significant difference between actualizing our life with love or remaining stuck.

Before we explore the way in which we can bring out the best use of our imagination, perhaps we should first examine the very elements that block us from experiencing this magnificent power.

Seven Fundamental Barriers That Block Our Imaginative Powers

1. Laziness

Sheer laziness has probably been responsible for more barriers that have blocked our imaginative powers than we are ready to admit—not to mention also how laziness decreases the valuable usage of the mind. The mind is a human organ, like any other, and without proper nutrition and exercise it can become sluggish and complacent.

Our environment can also contribute to a lazy and noncreative mind. Probably the greatest culprit depriving most of us from our creative processes is television. The A. C. Nielsen Co., which measures television audiences and their behavior, revealed that on average, in every American home the television set is on six hours and fourteen minutes per day. This is two hours more per day than the daily average in the 1960s, which is approximately the same point in time that SAT scores began to decline. This time frame is significant because the first generation to cut its teeth on TV began taking SATs in the early 1960s. *Media and Methods* reported that while the TV is on in the American home approximately twenty-one hundred hours per year, the average American spends only five hours per year reading books. Much can be said about the all-too-often toxic consequences of television and its unproductive effects on the human mind. It's a chilling fact when surveys indicate that 50 percent of Americans view television during dinner, and by the time one reaches the age of seventeen years, the average American child has logged fifteen thousand hours watching TV, the equivalent of two years . . . day and night! Television is not only a colossal waste of time, but it also causes the mind to sit idle and ultimately robs one from a vital, creative thinking process.

2. Fear

Fear is one of the deadliest barriers that can attack our imaginative faculty. Therefore, fear has a paralyzing effect on our creative thinking abilities. It is very difficult to think creatively while fear occupies your mind.

Fear of failure, fear that our ideas may appear foolish to others, fear of criticism, fear of success, and a myriad of other types of fear act as blockages. Perhaps one of the biggest blocks to exploring creativity resides in the fears that our ideas will be criticized. We can become afraid that we will not receive support. After all, if our ideas are new and have never been explored, such ideas can put you at risk of ridicule. The perception is that the more our ideas deviate from current norms and trends, the greater the chance of receiving a poor response to them. In seeking to protect fragile egos, many people prefer not to voice their ideas. These individuals would rather not even indulge in their creative daydreams to begin with! Most adults have a fear of looking foolish, which is one of the biggest hindrances to creative thinking, especially in a group setting. Have you ever been in a meeting and hesitated to speak up about the great idea that just popped into your head? We've all been there. We don't speak for fear of criticism.

Then there is also the fear that you are being set up for more failures by coming up with new ideas. While creativity gives us a chance for innovation, our ideas may turn out to be a success or a complete flop. "Wouldn't it be safer to stick to conventions or to old and tested ways?" many people reason. Fear of making mistakes can be a huge obstacle, preventing us from exploring creativity freely.

3. Environmental Distractions

Too much clutter can block the flow of creativity. Clutter can be both mental and physical.

In terms of mental clutter, creative ideas cannot flow freely if you are limited by thoughts of negativity, such as fear, blame, worry, or shame. Creativity is very difficult when our minds are constantly busy with—among many other things—a running internal monologue, making arrangements for our schedule, checking our email every two minutes, figuring how to make ends meet, and wondering whether to attend an event that we were asked to go to.

In terms of physical clutter, too much paper and other stuff lying around, as well as too many possessions, can be distracting. Clutter sucks the productivity right out of us, occupying our minds and leaving little or no space to explore creativity.

Then there is noise. Nonstop music, cars honking, and people chattering can also add to distraction and impede the imagination.

4. Quitting Early

Life is full of problems and challenges. The key is to put the mind to work, turning adversities into opportunities, but so many people don't even give themselves the time and the chance to do so.

The record for the shortest Major League Baseball career probably belongs to a member of the old Brooklyn Dodgers, a pitcher named Harry Hartman. He was a gifted young ballplayer whose day of glory arrived in 1918 when he was called up from the minors to pitch against the Pittsburgh Pirates. This was the moment he'd dreamed about, the beginning of a great career, but his dreams began to fade when his first pitch was hit for a single. The next batter tripled. Rattled, he walked the next batter on four straight pitches, and when he did throw a strike to the next hitter, it went for a single. At that point, Hartman had enough. He headed for the showers, dressed, and walked out of the stadium to a naval recruiting office, where he enlisted. The next day, he was in a military uniform, never to play professional baseball again.

If you suffer from low confidence, you may believe you are not capable. Hence, you choose to believe you are not able to come up with creative ideas. Do you think creativity is the domain of only geniuses, or of those who are smarter than you are? Limiting thoughts make great blocks to creativity. If you think that only special, talented people are creative and that geniuses are born and not made, then you may have no wish to develop your creative abilities.

5. Lack of Discipline

If you do not attach any importance to being creative, then you are not going to enjoy the benefits of being creative either.

Great composers do not sit down to work because they are inspired, but they become inspired because they are working. Beethoven, Wagner, Bach, and Mozart settled down day after day to the job in hand with as much regularity as an accountant settles down each day in his figures. Composer don't waste time waiting for inspiration.

6. Closed-Mindedness

A refusal to let go of one's existing thought pattern or narrow mind-set can limit a person's consideration of new possibilities. The more one limits oneself with irrelevant concepts or useless symbols, the more that creativity is stifled. The following story appeared in *Today in the Word*, and it addresses keeping one's mind open to a different way of thinking.

In 1937, architect Frank Lloyd Wright built a house for industrialist Hibbard Johnson. One rainy evening Johnson was entertaining distinguished guests for dinner when the roof began to leak. The water seeped through directly above Johnson himself, dripping steadily onto his bald head. Irate, he called Wright in Phoenix, Arizona.

"Frank," he said, "you built this beautiful house for me, and we enjoy it very much. But I have told you the roof leaks, and right now I am with some friends and distinguished guests and it is leaking right on top of my head."

Wright's reply was heard by all of the guests. "Well, Hib, why don't you move your chair?"

7. Lack of Rest

Inadequate sleep can hinder a person's creativity. The physical body needs to feel good before a person can develop and explore one's creative faculties.

* * *

Now that we have examined some items that hamper the creative process, let's look at five ways you can optimize the powers of your creative imagination.

Five Ways You Can Optimize the Powers of Your Creative Imagination

1. Claim Your Creative Self

You have an extraordinary ability to be creative; everybody does. That is the way we are made. You just need to simply take the challenge and look at situations and ways to bring it out in yourself.

When we think of creativity, we tend to picture a composer or an artist at work on a masterpiece. Instead, think of creativity as simply a new approach to anything.

Earle Dickson, an employee of Johnson & Johnson, married a young woman who was accident prone. Johnson & Johnson sold large surgical dressings in individual packages, but these were not practical for small cuts and burns. Dickson put a small wad of sterile cotton and gauze in the center of an adhesive strip to hold it in place. Finally, tired of making up these little bandages every time one was needed, he got the idea of making them in quantity and using crinoline fabric to temporarily cover the adhesive strip. When the bandage was needed, the two pieces of crinoline could easily be peeled off, producing a small, ready-to-use bandage.

The firm's president, James Johnson, saw Dickson put

one of his homemade bandages on his finger. Impressed by its convenience, he decided to start mass-producing them under the name Band-Aids. Dickson had been looking for a way to handle a small problem, and in the process he invented a useful new product.

2. Make Time for It

Creative thinking does not require a fancy place and time; it often comes throughout the day wherever you may be. Still, many people find it useful and productive to set out some time every day or week to try to exercise their creative faculties. Find some quiet time where you can engage your own thoughts. Take a break when you can tap into this part of yourself . . . it might even be in the shower!

Henry Ford was noted for saying, "A weakness of all human beings is trying to do too many things at once. That scatters effort and destroys direction. It makes for haste, and haste makes waste. So we do things all the wrong ways possible before we come to the right one. Then we think it is the best way because it works, and it was the only way left that we could see. Every now and then I wake up in the morning headed toward that finality, with a dozen things I want to do. I know I can't do them all at once."

When asked what he did about that, Ford replied, "I go out and trot around the house. While I'm running off the excess energy that wants to do too much, my mind clears and I see what can be done and should be done first."

3. Think outside the Box

If there ever was a term that has been synonymous with creative thinking, it is to "think outside the box." This phrase simply means to utilize your mind in an unconventional manner—to ask a lot of what, why, why not, or "what if" questions, and to stretch the mind and challenge the boundaries of conventional thinking. Children ask these types of questions all the time in such innocent ways, and they are not troubled by asking them.

Some examples:

Masaru Ibuka (honorary chairman, Sony) asked, Why don't we remove the recording function and speaker and put headphones in the recorder? From that question came the Sony Walkman!

Fred Smith asked, Why can't there be reliable overnight mail service? Challenging this simple but straightforward question led to the founding of Federal Express.

Godfrey Hounsfield asked, Why can't we see in three dimensions what is inside a human body without cutting it open? From that question came the invention of the CAT scan.

Bill Bowerman, the creator of Nike shoes, asked the outrageous question, What happens if I pour rubber into my waffle iron? From that question, Nike was born!

Many other individuals and companies dismissed these perspectives and thus missed extraordinary opportunities by overlooking their value.

Masaru Ibuka received comments like, "A recorder with no speaker and no recorder—are you crazy?"

Fred Smith didn't fair too well at Yale University when he proposed the idea of Federal Express—and got a less-than-impressive C for his efforts.

Godfrey Hounsfield was told the CAT scan was "impractical."

Other shoe companies thought Bowerman's waffle shoe was a "dumb idea."

Ridiculous, impossible, impractical—enough to discourage anyone! But these people, who achieved incredible status in their own fields, didn't let the critics stifle their creativity. Their questioning transformed business and science, bringing untold benefits and positive experiences to millions—and also causing these men to become wealthy and successful in the process.

4. Develop a Positive Self-Image

You are what you think you are! Maintaining a positive mind-set is essential to cultivating a bright, positive, can-do attitude, and it all begins in the imagination. The reality of the matter is that you don't need a remarkably high IQ to exercise an extraordinary imagination.

After physicist Richard Feynman won a Nobel Prize for his work, he visited his old high school. While there, he decided to look up his records. He was surprised to find that his grades were not as good as he had remembered them, and he got a chuckle out of the fact his IQ was 124, not very far above average. Dr. Feynman thought that winning the Nobel Prize was one thing, but winning it with an IQ of only 124 was really something else. Most of us would agree, because we all assume that the winners of Nobel Prizes in science have exceptionally high IQs.

Feynman confided he always knew he had a positive state of mind. But if Feynman had known he was really just a bit above average in the IQ department, perhaps he would not have had the audacity to launch the unique and creative research that would eventually win him the greatest recognition the scientific community can give. Maybe the knowledge that he was a cut above average, but not in the genius category, would have influenced what he tried to achieve. After all, from childhood most of us have been led to believe that ordinary people don't accomplish extraordinary feats.

Most of us fall short of our potential because of little things we know or assume about ourselves. The most self-defeating assumption of all might be that we are just like everyone else.

5. Write It Down

Finally, always be ready to write down your ideas. How many times has a good idea entered your mind, only to be forgotten a short time later? New ideas can come at any time. Record them when they do.

* * *

Exercising the power of the imagination is not only a vital and powerful means to breakthrough solutions but it is where and what dreams are made of. The difference between mediocrity and success lies in the center of your imagination.

A Point to Consider

Limitations are only the barriers we set in our own minds. If we use our imagination, the possibilities our endless!

Questions to Ponder

1. What creative idea have I used that has significantly and positively affected the way I do things?
2. What everyday activities can I engage in that will expand my imaginative capabilities?

8

FROM A FIRE TO A BONFIRE!

"Never doubt that a small group of thoughtful, committed citizens can change the world; indeed, it's the only thing that ever has."
—Margaret Mead

Every Tuesday at noontime is a very special time, as members of our GoalAchievers group meet to empower each other through the process of sharing our goals with one another.

This process is based on the premise that more can be accomplished in less time by working together in a spirit of cooperation and harmony. We realize that the whole is greater than the sum of the individual parts.

When individuals come together in this fashion, treating the needs of each member of the group as importantly as their own needs, something mysteriously powerful occurs. Many refer to it as synergy. In a case such as this, one and one do add up to two, but the combination of two or more energy forms result in an even greater force; a "third mind," so to speak, is developed.

For instance, consider when two individuals come together in a union of harmony and love with one another. Have you noticed that the combined force of a loving couple creates a dynamic that is substantially greater than the sum of the individuals? They accomplish more together because of this harmonious and loving union—a lot more than if they were independent from one another. So it is when two or more people even outside a romantic relationship are gathered in a spirit of complete trust, harmony, cooperation, and love. Very powerful dynamics take over, and tasks that might have seemed impossible now become achievable.

The late industrial tycoon Andrew Carnegie described it this way: "Teamwork is the ability to work together. It causes ordinary individuals to achieve extraordinary results."

How does this all work? What are some of the benefits and dynamics that occur when a group such as GoalAchievers gets together?

Through our weekly GoalAchievers group meeting we have discovered and experienced ten extraordinary benefits.

The Ten Outstanding Benefits of Being Part of a Personal Success Team

1. A Sense of Direction and Purpose

Every week when our group meets, we are constantly reminding co-members and ourselves of our definite chief aim. No longer is our quest toward achievement an individual effort, but now it becomes a group effort. All the members begin their sharing by stating their principal goal, the progress they have made with the help of other members, the challenges they face, and the continued action plan that is in place to reach the point of achievement. Through participation in the group, some members *discover* their chief goal and its purpose. With the group's help and encouragement, these members are able to find and establish a sense of direction and purpose for themselves. Other members arrive already knowing exactly what their purpose is, and through the collective effort of the group they are able to stay accountable and find the specific help they need to stay on track. Being part of a group keeps each member focused.

Set Yourself on Fire!

One of our group members admitted that for years she struggled to remain focused. The day she joined our group, however, she overcame this struggle. In her own words she states, "The GoalAchievers group is an amazing program that helped me to focus on important things and important goals. As a salesperson I have freedom to do whatever I want, and this program helps me with going after those goals, tasks, and activities that are the most important. Also, the weekly meetings ensure the regularity of focus."

2. Creative Thinking and Problem Solving

Have you ever been in a situation where you hit a mental roadblock? No matter how hard you tried, you just couldn't seem to get past a problem. Then someone came and put a little twist in your perspective, and "Voila!" your whole mode of thinking shifted. You were then able to make a substantial breakthrough, maybe even come up with could be a million-dollar idea.

That's exactly what happens in groups on a frequent basis. Members present their challenges in a trusted environment with one another, and the sparks begin to fly! If you think that two heads are better than one, how about five, seven, or ten minds all working at the same time to find a solution? How powerful is that?

Our group members combine to create a very powerful intelligence force that merges our collective thinking. Some in the group are Ph.D.s, MBAs, and CPAs; others are simply street-savvy. Nonetheless, when this collective brain-power goes to work, major breakthroughs in thinking occur and incredible achievements result. King Solomon noted the power of this kind of synergy when he wrote, "As iron sharpens iron, so one man sharpens another" (Proverbs 27:17).

Darrel rediscovered his creative gift and was set on fire.

Describing his experience, he referred to his fellow members "like the magic angels or characters of 'golden light' you see in the heart-warming movies. They are with light and advice just when the darkness of failure is about to envelop you! I cannot quantify the value of the service GoalAchievers has given me, and the 'jumpstart' given back to my writing career. My dreams and goals are back!"

3. An Instant and Valuable Support Network

Networking expert Harvey Mackay indicated that the average individual possesses a personal network of between 200 to 250 people. Often we overlook the power of tapping into our own network, but when we begin to list all the people we know, we may surprise even ourselves as to the enormity of our personal network. However, what happens when ten individuals come together to share their resources in a common quest to help one another? Suddenly, what was a network of 200 to 250 compounds to 2,000 to 2,500 people! What power! One of the great benefits derived constantly from our closely knit group is the power of our network. Certain members would never have had a chance of connecting with particular people. They now find themselves being able to make such connections because of the extent of our collective network. As a result, people are developing new and empowering relationships.

Dr. Martin Kijazi (and what a great man he is!) has been one of our long-lasting and loyal members. In examining the effectiveness of the group, he stated, "This initiative now allows many women and men to come together in harmonious cooperation to work as a team and help each other achieve their goals."

4. Extraordinary Opportunities

Of course, with this powerful and extended network, opportunities abound where otherwise there would be none. Certain career objectives and jobs are landed, financing is raised, expertise is sourced out, and sales are made. This bond of trust and referral allows the process of achievement to run more effectively and efficiently. Moreover, as a result of becoming part of a close-knit group such as GoalAchievers, everyone becomes one another's eyes and ears. In our particular case, where we have ten members in our group, instead of one simply having the use of two eyes and ears, members now have the use of twenty eyes and ears who are cognitive of one another's needs. They are always ready and on the lookout for one another, based on the awareness that is shared through our weekly meetings.

In short, the process is not limited to our meetings but is alive and active 24/7 as we call, email, and share information with each another on a daily basis.

Eva, who publishes an amazing newspaper called *Good News Toronto*, expresses her experience in being a part of a personal success team by saying that GoalAchievers is "an organization whose premise is that we all do our best work when we help each other. GoalAchievers encourages us to risk taking our personal journeys because we will be supported, encouraged, and helped along the way by other members of the group."

5. Inspiration

Something is extraordinarily inspiring when one group member sees another's progress and achievement! Through the sharing of ideas, resources, and specialized knowledge, members become inspired about each others' dreams. Hope abounds, and the positive energy that is generated inspires each member to achieve his or her dreams, goals, and objectives.

Another of our team members, Pubudu, found the inspiration he desperately needed in order to reach his dreams. He exclaimed, "GoalAchievers is a wonderful program for anybody who wants to achieve dreams and be successful. Phil has come up with a structured but practical mechanism to support achieving individual goals. Since I joined the GoalAchievers program a few months ago, I have started to visualize my goals more clearly. The feedback from others in the group is driving me to heights that I could not have imagined."

6. Encouragement

If we sorely need one thing in our lives as we pursue our dreams, it is encouragement. Too often in this world we are bombarded with negative messages. People are quick to point out how and why certain things cannot be done. Our GoalAchiever groups allow each member to enter a forum where encouragement abounds. Instead of being told why things can't be done, we are met with the empowering message of why and how they *can* be done! Let's face it: probably one of the greatest challenges for entrepreneurs and individuals who seek to do the extraordinary is that their great challenge can sometimes be discouraging.

The difference between success and failure can lie at the border of encouragement and discouragement. Henry David Thoreau observed, "The mass of men lead lives of quiet desperation," and they "go to the grave with the song still in them," as Oliver Wendell Holmes observed. However, those of us who gather in a spirit of close-knit unity, harmony, and cooperation do not resemble the masses. We are a community of individuals who put others in front of self, and in doing so we derive the great joy and reciprocal value of working together in a spirit of encouragement.

When one member feels discouraged we always have other members to pick him or her up. The encouragement we find from one another gives us the much-needed comfort and strength to keep pursuing our dream. The encouragement we find sometimes comes in the form of a simple phone call, meeting over a cup of coffee, a kind word, or practical and helpful solutions. One thing is certain: as a team we are there for one another, and no one is left to fend for themselves. We find our encouragement through each other.

Soojin was astounded when she first joined our group. She came in with doubts, but her experience has turned her into one of our most loyal members and biggest advocates of this process. Putting it succinctly she states, "I came in with some doubts and concerns, but the energy of all the members has lifted my spirit without any extra effort. Just come in and you will experience the magic."

7. Motivation

With the combined forces of inspiration and daily encouragement, we find strength for the journey, which translates into motivation. Our daily and weekly meetings provide a constant oasis for our members to find strength and inner resolve.

Every now and then, one of our group members will say, "I didn't really have the energy or feel like coming to the meeting today, but boy, am I ever glad I did! I feel so energized and motivated as a result." Never has a member of our group walked out of our meetings feeling worse than when they walked in. In fact, the very opposite is true. Our group sessions provide the motivation we all need to achieve our goals. Perhaps this is why we call ourselves GoalAchievers!

Claudia certainly discovered the value of being part of

our group: "The commitment to enhance and develop the best in others through our weekly GoalAchievers meetings and processes is truly empowering!"

8. Accountability

Have you ever set out to accomplish a goal, but lost sight of it not too long after? You may have let your goal slide because you didn't share it with anyone else. In losing sight of your goal, you deprived yourself of the benefits that come along with reaching it. One of the most powerful reasons to be part of a close-knit GoalAchiever team is the accountability factor. As a result of sharing our goals with one another, not only do we find encouragement, but each member also becomes accountable to one another. Among the key questions we ask of each other is, "What will you do from here to next week to draw closer to your goal?" This sense of accountability keeps everyone on their toes. Thus, each member becomes acutely aware of the commitment they have made to themselves and the group to follow through on their weekly action steps.

Another one of our group members was Clark, who, prior to joining our success team, struggled with the discipline needed to keep himself on track. Once Clark made the all-important decision to be part of our group, the results he was seeking began to show up in his life. Clark says, "GoalAchievers is great because it brings together, on a weekly basis, peers who will keep you accountable and on track. For myself, I was able to finally get a physical fitness routine going. As a result, I've not only lost weight, but I feel great and have found a new passion in running. It has gotten to the point where I'm keeping my eye out for running events to participate in and really take things to the next level. Thanks to the group for getting me on track."

9. Referrals and Endorsements

Networking and providing one another with valuable contacts and leads has certainly been one of the strong earmarks of being part of a success team. One of our team members recently introduced another member to what resulted in a $1 million contract.

The fact is that, everything being equal, people are more likely to do business with people whom they know, like, and trust. The camaraderie and trust that we establish among ourselves creates opportunities to meet other individuals and make significant progress within a very short period of time—progress that otherwise would take years to achieve. Although a success team is not, per se, officially a networking group, a strong networking component comes along with belonging to a success team. Networking is undoubtedly a vital skill that contributes to one's ability to achieve goals.

Individuals who could never have gotten face time with certain people now find themselves being introduced and sitting across the table from some of the most influential people in our country. It is truly astounding. We have had members introduced to CEOs, publishing magnates, celebrities, politicians, prominent authors, speakers, athletes, financiers, and myriad other professionals, individuals, and decision makers in almost every industry. Amazingly, it seems that through the power of our group there is hardly a person we cannot make arrangements for our members to meet. This is the power of a success team's networking. The fact of the matter is that this kind of networking power is available to almost anyone who sees the value and benefit of working together as a team, rather than attempting to tread down the road of life alone.

10. Measurable Progress and Results

Finally, success teams are enormously beneficial simply because they work! There is no denying the substantial process, growth, and achievement that having your own personal success team produces. So successful is this approach that no one who has consistently gone our path has ever fallen short of achieving significant process. Members of our group admitted that for years prior to joining, they might have thought about accomplishing certain goals, but the time would go by without any movement or progress. However, the moment they decided to embrace being part of a team in the quest to achieve their goals, they achieved what they always wanted to achieve. The confidence, encouragement, support, and accountability they found in the group truly made the difference!

One of our most dynamic members, upon reflection, encapsulated his experience in these terms: "GoalAchievers is a holy and energetic place where sparks of our dreams become the fire of our passions. It's a place where people help each other through the kindness of their hearts in the spirit of love and giving. It provides a place where one can find inspiration or support of great like-minded people, and resources that act as catalysts to speed up the journey of its members toward the goals of their lives. If anyone is interested in building a support network or finding direction and encouragement in an honest and loving environment, GoalAchievers is the place you can't miss. If someone added one or ten more years to your life by simply speeding up your journey toward your goals, what value would you put on that? That's what you can expect when you join GoalAchievers."

In summary, we have been fortunate enough to belong to a mastermind group called GoalAchievers. This is our success team. However, one does not have to be a member of GoalAchievers in particular to catapult yourself toward the achievement of your dreams and goals, although you are certainly welcome to join us. But finding and becoming part of a success team is vital if you are going to truly reach the heights of your dreams. Success is a team sport, no matter how you look at it. The question becomes, what success team do you belong to?

The following inspirational story has been disseminated widely on the Internet:

> At the Seattle Special Olympics a few years ago, nine contestants, all physically or mentally disabled, gathered at the starting line for the hundred-yard dash. At the gun they all started out, not exactly in a dash, but with the enthusiasm to run the race to the finish and win. One boy stumbled on the asphalt, though. He tumbled over a couple of times and began to cry. The other eight heard the boy cry. They slowed down and paused. Then they all turned around and went back . . . every one of them. One girl with Down syndrome bent down, kissed him, and said, "This will make it better." Then all nine linked arms and walked together to the finish line. Everyone in the stadium stood, and the cheering went on for ten minutes.

In many ways, this is exactly what happens when you are part of closely knit success team.

One of the fundamental building blocks to success is the ability to harness the power of cooperative effort toward the achievement of a common goal.

This is at the heart of any successful mastermind group!

The basic premise of our GoalAchiever groups—or any mastermind group, for that matter—is that more can be accomplished in less time by working together in a spirit of harmony and cooperation.

Set Yourself on Fire!

The word "team" has also been frequently used as an acronym meaning, "*Together Everyone Accomplishes More!*"

The lives of some of the most notable achievers in history show often that their success resulted from the keen ability to gain the cooperation of others.

Don Shula, who holds the record for the most wins of any coach in NFL history, was once asked about the secret to his success. His answer: "I try to find out as much as I can about every player on my team and then try to get the most out of him and blend these talents into a team."

There's no question that the virtue of a genuinely caring attitude toward others has a contagious effect. Once we have discovered and ignited our own personal flame, we can turn our fire into a bonfire by working with others as a team!

A Point to Consider

The letters in the word "team" can stand for "Together Everyone Accomplishes More!"

Questions to Ponder

1. What success team do you belong to?
2. What benefits have you derived or can you derive by being part of a success team?

9

THE CORNERSTONE OF SUCCESS!

"If you want 1 year of prosperity, grow grain. If you want 10 years of prosperity, grow trees. If you want 100 years of prosperity, grow people."
—Chinese Proverb

Howard Schultz, founder of Starbucks coffee, is certainly one of the more notable individuals to set himself on fire with his dream! From his humble beginnings in Seattle during the early 1980s, Howard Schultz took his vision and expanded it with all the zeal one could muster up. By the time he hit the 1990s, Starbucks was opening a new store every workday, a pace that continued into the 2000s. It has become very rapidly the largest coffee house company in the world, with (as of the time of this writing) 16,635 stores in 49 countries. Despite some recent challenges, Starbucks remains the gold standard for this type of business.

What's remarkable is that he did this without having to franchise his business. How did he do it? What is at the core of his philosophy that makes Starbucks so successful?

Although more than one component goes into success stories, one cornerstone usually sets the foundation for growth, and that is people.

Frequently you hear Howard say in his interviews, "We are not in the coffee business serving people, but in the people business serving coffee." What an empowering philosophy! And when Howard speaks it, one can immediately sense that he means it with all his heart. This core value has made Starbucks what it is.

Set Yourself on Fire!

Interestingly enough, recently I had met a friend at a local Starbucks. Seeing her already seated, I rushed over to greet her, and we began speaking. I had completely lost track of getting a coffee. However, not too long into our conversation, a wonderful man draped in a Starbucks' apron came over to me with a great big smile and a cup of coffee in hand and said, "Here, sir! Thought you might enjoy this?"

Wow! That was exactly what I wanted! How did he know? I turned around and said, "Why, thanks so much. How much will that be?"

He then replied, with a warm and kind demeanor, "Oh no, sir. This is on the house!"

Well, that just made my day. The funny thing is, he didn't know me from a hole in the ground, and little did he know that I would eventually be writing about and alluding to this random act of kindness to my audiences around the globe. Needless to say, though, because of this small, thoughtful, yet very meaningful act, I have become a loyal and strong proponent of Starbucks.

Shortly thereafter, I happened to be listening to an interview with Howard Schultz on the Charlie Rose show, and sure enough I heard his mantra: "We're not in the coffee business serving people, we're in the people business serving coffee."

The Starbucks philosophy was alive and well, and it had trickled down into the hearts and minds of their associates on the front lines.

Starbucks is another core example of what I deal with in the next chapter: how companies and individuals can win others over by going the second mile.

What creates this exceptional type of behavior? Is it mere mechanics, or is it that people who are successful are equipped with something a little deeper?

It's been said that most of our happiness and success in business and life depends on how well we learn to get along with others. On the other hand, it was once noted, he who cannot get along with people has earned the kiss of death. People are all we have! One's ability to interact in a positive and effective way with others is clearly the single most important skill one can possess.

So let's begin! How can one harness this great skill of human relations?

There are two fundamental components: Understanding the do's and don'ts of human relations and bringing out the best of one's own inner character.

If we learn to look within ourselves and seek to improve our own character, the mechanics have a way of falling into place. If one attempts to focus only on etiquette and not on one's own character, the process of winning people over with a pleasant personality is just mechanics and nothing more.

For one to truly harness the skill of getting along with others, one must start from the inside and let the essence of one's own being naturally express itself in an outward fashion.

If an individual tries to be genuinely interested in others, and yet does not possess a genuine heart that *is* interested in others, this lack of sincerity will eventually reveal itself.

To act in a truly becoming manner, one must have a truly becoming character. That is the starting point of all successful human interactions.

One cannot act against one's own nature—at least not for long. For instance, if you take an orange and you squeeze it, what comes out? Orange juice, right! Or if you take an apple and run it through a juicer, what comes out? Yes, apple juice! So it is with the human soul. Whatever essence we carry inside, whenever we are squeezed, whether it is "good or bad," that is exactly what will emerge in our words and in our conduct.

Individuals who are genuinely happy don't have to try to

be happy. They just are. By the same token, someone who is unhappy can try and smile and exude warmth, but their insincerity becomes apparent to others and the opposite effect takes place. For instance, have you ever seen someone with a fake smile? Don't you agree that it would be better if they didn't try to smile at all?

Now that we have set this very important premise, what are some of the life-enhancing attitudes that can truly make you a person who is attractive to others?

The answer can be found in this one powerful word: love. And not just any kind of love, but a deep, sincere love that hopes all things, believes all things—a love that conquers all.

We hear the word "love" so often that we can become confused or desensitized to its true meaning. For instance, we use the word "love" for a wide range of applications. We can say we love pizza, baseball, or photography. We can say we love our dog or our work, and of course we can expand the very same word to mean we love our kids, family, or spouse.

What does the word "love" really mean?

One of the limitations of language is that one word can take on myriad meanings. However, to really understand the meaning of the word "love," perhaps we should examine the three ancient Greek terms for it, which define love with greater precision.

Three Types of Love Defined

Philia

One term for love that the ancient Greeks used was *philia*, which referred to a brotherly love, including friendship and affection toward those whom we are naturally inclined to like. This term gave birth to the name of the city Philadelphia, which is referred to as the city of brotherly love. All of us have, and continue to experience, this type of love in our everyday lives.

Eros

Another term the ancient Greeks used to describe love was *eros*, from which we derive the modern-day English word "erotic." This word implied a certain type of love that you would find between a loving couple. It is a sensual, romantic type of love. Most human beings experience or have experienced this type of love at some point in their lives. It is a very human, common type of love.

Agape

Agape in the ancient Greek referred to a godly type of love that is love in the purest sense of the word: the most supreme form of love, a rare type of love that when discovered and experienced would represent the most powerful essence on earth.

This type of love was first recorded in ancient Greek scrolls. The Bible describes *agape* in these vivid terms.

"Love is patient and kind.

Love is not jealous or boastful or proud or rude.

It does not demand its own way.

It is not irritable, and it keeps no record of being wronged.

It does not rejoice about injustice but rejoices whenever the truth wins out.

Love never gives up,

Never loses faith,

Is always hopeful,

And endures through every circumstance."

(1 Corinthians 13:4–7)

Set Yourself on Fire!

To emphasize the supremacy of this great life-enhancing virtue, Scripture summarizes the description with these words:

"Three things will last forever—faith, hope, and love—and the greatest of these is love" (1 Corinthians 13:13).

Can you imagine if we all possessed this kind of love? We wouldn't need the military, law enforcement, prisons, judges, or even lawyers. You heard me right: no lawyers! Everyone would get along with one another, and we would be living in complete harmony. Moreover, there would be no hunger, domestic abuse, war, environmental crises, or any number of other tragedies in our world today.

In short, *love* is the answer!

However, this is not the world we live in. For one reason or another, many people have taken a different path in life.

But here's the point: if this *agape* love could bring such healing and harmony into our world, could you imagine what it would do for your ability to interact in the most positive way with others? We cannot control how other people choose to live, but we always have within our own personal reach a solution that allows us to choose and live a higher form of life if we so desire.

The fact is, once we can tap into this essence, all those things we read about how to effectively and positively interact with others would not be something for which we would have to discipline ourselves to remember. Rather, it would naturally flow out of the expressions of our hearts.

As the proverb of old states, "As he thinks in his heart so is he" (Proverbs 23:7).

As we move along in this chapter, we recap some well-documented human relations skills that are truly wonderful and commendable. By following these principles, we can live happier and more successful lives. While we can try to live up to these principles using our own will, an easier approach is to let this wonderful essence of *agape* love flow in and through us in a manner that is effortless and natural.

A powerful, all-encompassing summary of effective interpersonal communication can be found in the phrase I mentioned earlier in the book: "People don't care how much you know, until they know how much you care!"

If there is any way to summarize how to interact with others effectively, it is found in this profound truth and virtue called caring. Once people know that you genuinely and sincerely care about them even more than your own needs, you will see the barriers come down and the gates of mutual understanding and success begin to occur.

In a seemingly nonchalant and indifferent world where the majority of people are preoccupied with their own needs, the people who win out are the ones who can genuinely express a caring spirit. And what better way to demonstrate and cultivate a genuinely caring attitude than to fully embrace this virtue called *agape* love?

Ever since the publication of the inspiring, landmark book titled *How to Win Friends and Influence People* by Dale Carnegie, many similar books have been written extolling life-enhancing principles of positive and effective communication.

In an interview with best-selling author Stephen Covey, Larry King asked him basically, "Stephen, your book is so inspiring, attracting the readership of millions, yet the principles are nothing new. They have been around since the beginning of time, haven't they? What makes this book such a success?"

If the works of people like Dale Carnegie, Stephen Covey, and many others seem to be so basically simple and full of so much common sense, one can only wonder if maybe "common sense" isn't really all that common. Perhaps it should be rephrased, as one of my friends once observed, as "not so common, common sense."

Isn't it obvious that we ought to praise rather than criticize? Smile rather than frown? Remember people's names and birthdays? Give thanks rather than complain? Take a genuine interest in others rather than merely look out for our own interests? In essence, shouldn't we exercise the Golden Rule in all our affairs? This lists just a few basic courtesies of effective human relations.

Why must these principles even need to be taught?

Yes, these principles are very much worth studying, for they inspire the heart and spur us to better and more harmonious relations with others. However, we can study these principles until we are blue in the face, but if we do not practice them with heartfelt authenticity, these principles risk becoming mere tactics or motions we go through rather than sincere expressions of the heart.

Effective communication with others goes much deeper than niceties and surface expressions of proper and conscientious conduct. It is in essence a matter of the heart.

If anything, these wonderful principles of human relations ought to serve as a mirror, validating the condition of one's own character and heart, rather than an outer attempt to develop good character. To attempt exercising such principles without a character steeped in goodness is nothing more than mere cosmetics.

In inviting and embracing the truest essence of love into our lives, we won't have to remember to smile in order to make a good impression. We will smile because it will flow naturally out of the expression of who we are.

We won't have to make a special effort to remember important dates, birthdays, anniversaries, and so forth. It will come naturally because our disposition will be one of courtesy and thoughtfulness. Remembering people's names, expressing gratitude, and genuinely caring about others will come easily and naturally.

We won't have to remember to take a deep interest in others and their needs by putting their needs before our own, because this will be who we are.

We won't have to find ways to demonstrate we care, because caring will shine through naturally in everything we say and do.

How would you feel or respond to someone, whether in business or everyday life, who expressed this kind of love toward you? Would you have a tendency to like them? Would you trust them? Would you want to engage and give them your business and your time?

The irony is that when a person discovers and lives by this all-encompassing and powerful virtue, joy and success become inevitable!

Somehow I do not feel compelled to tell anyone they should find this kind of love. That would be awfully presumptuous. I can only share with you my own experience.

Often when we refer to a person's imperfections or faults we say, "Well, he's human!" Why is the term "being human" equated with imperfection? At least in my situation, it's because the equation applies perfectly.

Looking deep within my own soul, I realize that there are elements of fear, pride, and selfishness, and ultimately I need ongoing help from a greater source to overcome these character defects and shortcomings. For myself, I had no other choice but to appeal to the God of all creation to empower me to become a person who would reflect the essence of the purest meaning of *agape* love. In moments of quiet prayer and meditation I have discovered the source of this great love. And perhaps, although I am a work in progress, I can express this kind of love to others in my speech and in my conduct.

May I encourage and suggest that should you find yourself at a crossroad similar to what I have had to battle, you appeal to the One who can and will make this transformation in your heart. If I have discovered one thing, it is that God is love! God is the very source of these life-giving attributes that can make each of us fully into a person who reflects a life set on fire—a positive force for good in our own lives and all with whom we come into contact.

If you feel something stirring within yourself right now, may I encourage you to take this moment to pause and just talk to God? Tell everything! Pour your heart out to Him—your fears, your doubts, and your uncertainties. Be still, and let God speak back to your heart. Talk to Him, and let Him talk to you, and in doing so you will discover a realm of understanding that you may have never experienced.

People have said, "I'll see it, *then* I'll believe it." But in the spiritual realm, you will see it *when* you believe it.

May God bless you!

A Point to Consider

People don't care how much you know, until they know how much you care.

Questions to Ponder

1. When I get "squeezed" by the pressures and challenges of life, what comes out?
2. What activity can I incorporate in my everyday life that will empower me to interact more successfully with others?

10

GOING THE SECOND MILE!

"There are no traffic jams in the second mile."
—Anonymous

If one mark confirms that people have truly set themselves on fire, it is that they are so enthusiastic, so excited, and so passionate about what they do that they are constantly delivering and doing more than what is expected of them. This activity comes from a heart of sheer love and enthusiasm about what they do and their eagerness to share it with others.

During the time of Christ, the Roman Empire governed the land. There was a decree that made it mandatory for the people to carry the baggage of a Roman soldier for one mile whenever they were asked. The soldiers by law could make this request at any time, but they could not demand that their baggage be carried for more than one mile.

This law had created and fueled a sense of resentment among the people whose land the Romans occupied. However, Jesus taught his disciples what seemed to be a peculiar series of instructions, which included not resisting abuse, but to actually do good to those who mistreated them. As Jesus spoke on the Mount of Olives he stated these words: "You have heard that it was said, 'An eye for an eye and a tooth for a tooth.' But I tell you not to resist an evil person. But whoever slaps you on your right cheek; turn the other to him also. If anyone wants to sue you and take away your tunic, let him have your cloak also." And finally He went on to say, "Whoever compels you to go one mile, go with him two!" (Matthew 5:41).

Set Yourself on Fire!

Thus we find the origins of the saying, "Go the extra mile."

In Jesus' day, the general consensus was to simply repay good for good, and evil for evil. To go beyond the boundaries of logical justice was unheard of. But what was it that propelled those who followed this revolutionary teaching to go the second mile?

The answer was simple and obvious. Love—a powerful passion to embrace a new value system and follow the principles of Christ. This great passion compelled Jesus' disciples to not just drop the bags, as they had the right by law to do after the first mile, but rather to go a second mile.

The Roman soldiers were so impressed by this incredible act of benevolence that they obviously could not resist inquiring what prompted these self-sacrificing and passionate individuals to act in such a manner. This was the beginning of an opportunity for Christ's disciples to share the reason behind their actions.

In the latter part of the Roman Empire, the Roman soldiers were the ones to spread most of Christianity. Christ's disciples had set themselves on fire, and that fire caught on with the Roman soldiers. Consequently, the Roman soldiers were set ablaze with this new revolutionary message, which they spread throughout the ruling empire and beyond.

When you set yourself on fire, people clearly see a difference in you. They will witness that your service to them is not based on mere obligation or a quest to make money but out of a genuine heart of love for what you are doing.

In essence, going the second mile means delivering more than what is required or expected. The motive is passion, and yet the by-product of this philosophy is revolutionary. Companies and individuals adapting this powerful mind-set and approach to their services are the very ones who become the leaders in their field.

One such company is Avis Car Rental, which in 1962

decided to make going the extra mile their core operating philosophy. Wrapped around a powerful new slogan, "We Try Harder!" and a strong commitment to expressing this value in everything they did, Avis's sales and position in the industry suddenly soared.

Before 1962 Hertz was the clear leader in the car rental business, with Avis as one of the brands in the following pack. The Avis "We Try Harder!" campaign repositioned Hertz, creating a relative, believable, and compelling strength for Avis. Hertz's market dominance became a weakness, and Avis became the right choice in the minds of consumers.

The results were dramatic.

In 1962, just before the first "We Try Harder" ads were launched, Avis was an unprofitable company with 11 percent of the U.S. car rental business. Within a year of launching the campaign, Avis was making a profit, and by 1966 Avis had tripled its market share to 35 percent.

Dominos Pizza founder Thomas Monaghan believed in delivering more than what was expected. Driven by this core value, what was originally a small pizza shop in an obscure town in Michigan had now gained a reputation for excellence. With its policy of delivering pizza in 30 minutes or it's free, Dominos quickly grew and spread into the second-largest pizza chain in the world. This approach to customer service excellence was so successful that it revolutionized the pizza delivery business. Consequently, myriads of pizza companies have attempted to emulate Dominos' philosophy since its inception, but none has achieved the level of success of its originator.

In July 1962 a visionary by the name of Sam Walton opened up a department store on 719 Walnut Street in Rogers, Arkansas. He called the store Wal-Mart. Walton was equipped with extraordinary knowledge that came through trial and error from his previous ventures. Because of his unwavering commitment to exceed customer expectations, Sam Walton built a worldwide empire of stores.

Within five years, Wal-Mart expanded to 24 stores across Arkansas. In 1968 the expansion continued as Wal-Mart opened its first stores outside Walton's home state. As Wal-Mart grew with a remarkable success rate from the 1960s into the 1980s, it had 1,198 stores and sales of $15.9 billion with 200,000 associates.

Today Wal-Mart is everywhere! In fact, Wal-Mart's presence in the United States alone is so prevalent that only a few small pockets of the country remained no further than 60 miles from the nearest Wal-Mart. Moreover, it is the largest retailer and private employer in America, with over 3,800 stores in the United States and 2,800 elsewhere, employing more than 1.6 million associates worldwide, with staggering annual sales of over $401.2 billion!

Who would have known that this unknown entrepreneur with a single store in a relatively remote part of the country would spearhead what would become the largest corporation in the world? Sam Walton also became one of the wealthiest men in the world.

What was Sam Walton's secret? Wal-Mart's success philosophy was formulated and built into Walton's character way before the first Wal-Mart store was ever erected.

In 1945, to be specific, Sam Walton dreamed of owning a department store. With a small amount of personal savings and money borrowed from his father-in-law, Sam embarked upon opening his first store. Due to limited funds at the time, he initially settled for a variety store. Here Walton pioneered many concepts that would prove to be crucial to his success. Walton made sure the shelves were consistently stocked with a wide range of goods at low prices. His store also stayed open later than most other stores, especially during the Christmas season. He also pioneered the practice of discount merchandising by buying wholesale goods from the lowest-priced suppliers and passing on the savings to his customers, which consequently drove up his sales volume.

Most important, Sam Walton lived by an all-encompassing creed.

One of his cornerstone philosophies—as outlined in his biography, *Made in America*—was simple but powerful! Simplicity in all things, "Deliver more than you promise!"

Study the successful individuals and companies that have passed the test of time, and you will find one outstanding quality: they consistently did more than what was expected, always going the extra mile.

What causes these people and industry leaders to go the second mile? Is it a mere act of corporate and personal discipline, or is there more to it?

The answer comes back to the core message of this book: If you are to live a life that is set on fire, you deliver excellence in everything you do. Moreover, you must have a burning passion for what you do in life.

Once you have caught the fire, obtained a burning desire and a zeal for what you are doing, and have gone the second mile, doing more than what you are paid for naturally falls into place. Whether your life calling is to be a writer, speaker, architect, accountant, engineer, scientist, artist, or housewife, whatever you love doing, you will most likely excel at it! At the very least, you'll excel much more than if you were doing something that you didn't enjoy—like simply doing it to earn a living and pay the bills.

Here's the bottom line. Do what you love, and the money will follow! Sadly, most people have it backward. They do what they don't like in order to earn money. They then try to use the money to buy their happiness and comfort. But in reality the approach ought to be to do what you love first, and then find a creative way to turn your passion, your labor of love, into a service that people would be more than willing to purchase. Life is too short to be doing anything other than what you are absolutely passionate for, isn't it?

When you love what you do, your labor is not laborious at all, but rather a beautiful expression of your God-given talents and abilities. Working those extra hours that can often put us ahead of our counterparts comes easy, and finding that extra energy to bring about endurance, which brings one to achievement, is no problem. All this flows effortlessly when we are involved in doing what we love.

Best-selling author Harvey Mackay put it succinctly when he stated, "Do what you love, and you will never have to work another day in your life!"

We all have unique gifts and abilities. If they are harnessed in the right direction, you can translate a seemingly ordinary existence into an extraordinary life!

Taking It a Notch Higher!

Then there are people who do what they love because they have adopted an attitude that is elevated beyond the physical task at hand. They do what they love simply because of whom they serve! Their employer has created such exemplary leadership and has earned such respect and devotion from the workforce that working for that employer is a labor of love.

When we are motivated by this awesome power called love, our work is not laborious but an expression of this life-enhancing virtue. Love for your work, love for your employer, love for your family, love for life, and most important, love for God!

One might call this reaching a spiritual realm of service. In his letter to the Colossians, Saint Paul wrote, "What so ever you do, do it heartily as unto God and not as unto man" (3:23). For those who have discovered a love for God and His goodness and grace, it is easy to work joyfully. It is easy to understand that everything we do, big or small, has tremendous significance in light of labor that is expressed in an attitude of love. Inevitably, when one discovers and experiences this, then going the second mile is an element that easily and naturally falls into place. With this principle comes enormous blessings, promotions, and advancements.

This principle was eloquently expressed by the late Martin Luther King Jr., when he stated, "Everybody can be great, because anybody can serve. You don't have to have a college degree to serve. You don't have to make your subject and verb agree to serve. You only need a heart full of grace. A soul generated by love."

Then he went on to say, "If a man is called to be a street sweeper, he should sweep streets even as Michelangelo painted, or Beethoven composed music, or Shakespeare wrote poetry. He should sweep streets so well that all the hosts of heaven and earth will pause to say, here lived a great street sweeper who did his job well!"
One cannot help but get the chills when hearing the immortal words of this great thinker and orator.

Martin Luther King Jr. clearly reflected a deeper sense of meaning and the nobility and worthiness of a labor conducted in a spirit of love. The work that he exhorted his listeners to do had significance and promoted a sense of excellence because it served a higher purpose.

Ralph Waldo Emerson, in his great essay titled "Compensation," put it this way: "If you serve an ungrateful master serve him the more. Put God in your debt. Every stroke shall be repaid. The longer the payment is withheld the better for you, for compound interest on compound interest, the rate of this exchequer." Emerson also wrote in that essay, "The law of Nature is do the thing and you shall have the power; but they who do not do the thing have not the power. . . . Men suffer all their life long, under the foolish superstition that they can be cheated. But it is as impossible for a man to be cheated by anyone but himself, as for a thing to be, and not to be, at the same time. There is a third silent party to all our bargains. The nature and soul of things takes on itself the guarantee of fulfillment of every contract, so that honest service can not come to loss."

Summarizing this unavoidable law, Emerson states, "It is one of the beautiful compensations of this life that no man can sincerely try to help another without helping himself."

Moreover, when one combines this spiritual and winning attitude with one's unique and special gifts, watch out, world! Because that particular person will have set himself and the world on fire!

So what are we saying here?

Do what you love, and love what you do. Whatever your hand finds to do, do it joyfully with all your might. Find ways to always deliver more than what you are paid for, or what is expected from you.

For example, if your employer expects you to work from nine to five, try coming in at eight and leaving at six. If a customer asks you for a particular product or service, find a way to give more than what was expected or requested—a little extra or even a lot extra! In all things and in all ways, find ways to pleasantly surprise people by being generous with your time, efforts, and resources.

In a world filled with mediocrity, a mind-set that all too often prevails holds that one should try to get away with getting more than what one puts out. Your spirit and attitude of going the second mile will make you stand out in a crowd, and you cannot help but be recognized and rewarded for your generosity.

Napoleon Hill, legendary researcher on the science of achievement and author of the best-selling book *Think and Grow Rich*, put it this way: "You need have no fear of competition from the person who says, 'I'm not paid to do this and I'll not do it.' He will never be a dangerous competitor for your job. But watch out for the fellow who remains at his work until it is finished and performs a little more than is expected of him, for he may challenge you at the post and pass you at the grandstand."

In everything you do, you may want to ask yourself, *How can I do this better? What can I do to deliver more than what is required and expected of me? How can I go the second mile in relation to the task that is before me?*

You will discover that cultivating this great habit is not only a virtuous expression of your labor in and of itself, but it also makes good business sense. It is a powerful means to add joy to your own life and others, and the quintessential means that separates the good from great, thus putting you on the top of your game.

Going the second mile is the great secret of success!

A Point to Consider

One of the beautiful compensations of this life is that no man can sincerely try to help another without helping himself.

Questions to Ponder

1. When and where did you experience someone going the second mile for you? What kind of impression did it leave with you?
2. How can I go the second mile in relation to the people I serve each day?

11

THE FLAME THAT KEEPS ON BURNING

*"But seek ye first the kingdom of God and His righteous-
ness and all these things will be added unto you."*
—Matthew 6:33

Now that you have set yourself on fire, how do you keep
the flame burning? There is no question that a life that
is set ablaze and keeps on burning is one that is consumed
with offering that life up in loving service to others. Life is
exciting and exhilarating when we find our true calling and
live with passion. We all have powerful and unique gifts to
offer up to others. It is just a matter of finding what that special gift is and having the courage and the faith to pursue
what innately is in each one of us. As I consider my own faith,
I discover the life-enhancing words of Christ, who declared,
"I have come to give you life and life more abundantly" (John
10:10). That means a life that is full and meaningful!

My place is not to force upon others what they should or
should not believe in. People decide to believe in what they
so desire and choose. All I can do is share with you what has
given me a sense of true hope, strength, and meaning. In
fact, for me not to do so would be to neglect the most important message in this book.

What does it means to have a life that is set on fire?

One man who certainly was ablaze with his purpose and
mission was the late Dr. Martin Luther King Jr. On April 3,
1968, he delivered his famous "I've Been to the
Mountaintop" speech—a message of passion, faith, and
courage. He spoke in what appeared to be prophetic terms.

Set Yourself on Fire!

Toward the end of the speech King refers to threats against his life and uses language that seems to foreshadow his impending death. Standing behind a lectern in a church in Memphis, Tennessee, he spoke these words:

"And then I got to Memphis. And some began to say the threats, or talk about the threats that were out. What would happen to me from some of our sick white brothers? Well, I don't know what will happen now. We've got some difficult days ahead. But it doesn't matter with me now. Because I've been to the mountaintop! And I don't mind. Like anybody, I would like to live a long life. Longevity has its place. But I'm not concerned about that now. I just want to do God's will. And He's allowed me to go up to the mountain. And I've looked over. And I've seen the promised land. I may not get there with you. But I want you to know tonight, that we, as a people, will get to the promised land. So I'm happy tonight. I'm not worried about anything. I do not fear any man. Mine eyes have seen the glory of the coming of the Lord!"

A day later, on April 4 Martin Luther King Jr.'s physical life came to an abrupt end as he was hit by an assassin's bullet. His physical life came to an end, but his flame kept on burning just as strongly, if not more so, and still keeps burning on to this day. There is no doubt that it is a sad and unjust way for a man to die. However, even though his enemies attempted to extinguish the flame, the fire blazes on.

Fortunately, most of us will not have to lay down our own lives for the sake of our dream.   However, if there is any secret to real success, it is in finding and committing yourself to a cause that is so great that it will even outlive your own existence! This is the ultimate expression of not only a life that has been set on fire but one that will keep on burning far after your physical body is gone.

How did Martin Luther King Jr. respond to his impending death? In a pretty startling fashion, actually. Remember his words: "I don't mind. Like anybody, I would like to live a long life. Longevity has its place. But I'm not concerned about that now. I just want to do God's will. . . . I'm not worried about anything. I'm not fearing any man."

Strange as this may seem, when one lives on with a purpose, there is a great sense of peace that comes.

Most people don't like to talk about death. And I can hear the response already: "Oh, Phil, you're going to talk about death, are you?" Oh, yes, I will. Because to those who live a life that is immersed in truthfulness and love, death is actually good news. Death is just as much an important and exciting part of life as being born. And let's face it: we are going to go down that road at some point.

Most people dread that thought, but one need not do so—not if one is secure in the knowledge of who they are as a child of God.

Saint Paul expressed the balance of life and death eloquently when he stated, "For me to live is Christ, and to die is gain!" (Philippians 1:21). What was he saying? First, at the time this remarkable man Paul penned these words, he was facing the prospect of death on an ongoing basis, much like Martin Luther King Jr. faced it. Paul didn't have it easy, to say the least.

In fact, a short synopsis of the latter part of Paul's life is astounding when one considers what he endured. Here is a partial account of the adversity he faced: "I've worked much harder, been jailed more often, beaten up more times than I can count, and at death's door time after time. I've been flogged five times with the Jews' thirty-nine lashes, beaten by Roman rods three times, pummeled with rocks once. I've been shipwrecked three times, and immersed in the open sea for a night and a day. In hard traveling year in and year out, I've had to ford rivers, fend off robbers, struggle with friends, struggle with foes. I've been at risk in the city, at risk in the country, endangered by desert sun and sea storm, and betrayed by those I thought were my brothers. I've known drudgery and hard labor, many a long and lonely night without sleep, many a missed meal, blasted by the cold, naked to the weather. And that's not the half of it!" (2 Corinthians 11:23–28).

Wow! What a life! And I find myself complaining about having to stand in line at the bank?

The point is that this great man was well acquainted with the possibilities of death on a constant basis. But like Martin Luther King Jr. so eloquently expressed, he still wanted to live. He was a man on a mission, a soul that had definitely set himself on fire!

And so what was his attitude during all of that? Complete joy. In fact, in his writings he indicates to his readers to rejoice always. And just in case they didn't understand it the first time, he repeated himself, "and again I say rejoice!" (Philippians 4:4).

You see, Saint Paul and other exceptional individuals who had gone before him and who came after him were not moved by circumstances but rather by an inner strength, belief, and conviction. Everything could be taken away from him, but one thing his foes did not and could not take from him was the power and the strength that lived and breathed within him.

He was a joyful soul—a man consumed with love, faith, and passion regardless of the circumstances. And why? Because of Christ! He goes on to say that for him to live is the embodiment and experience of what it is to live in the inextinguishable power, glory, and strength of Jesus. It was an experience of sheer internal bliss, and so he enjoyed living, regardless of the outward trials. Now, one can say many things, but I submit to you that one who can live like this is the strongest, richest, and most successful person alive.

Saint Paul went on to say, in so many words, that if this frustrates my enemies so that they even decide one day to kill me, that's great! It's as if he was saying, "I want to live, but if you so choose to kill me, I still win! In fact, not only do I win, but also, I gain!" Why gain? Because he was so completely at peace with the knowledge of where he was going at the transition of his death.

How many of us can say that? Are you secure in terms of where you are going in the afterlife? Do you have the same sense of confidence and peace about the afterlife as did Saint Paul and Martin Luther King Jr.?

Would you like to?

How does an individual come to this incredible place of internal security, joy, and serenity? Is it possible?

Some of you may be saying to yourselves, "I just don't know. I'd like to know, but I don't know. I try to be good, but I don't know if it's going to cut it. I still don't have that overwhelming peace and security."

Some of us may be too acutely aware of our own imperfections and wrongs. Buried in guilt, shame, and fear, we are having difficulty even forgiving ourselves. We try to bury the thoughts with various means of distraction.

May I suggest that the questions of life and death are not to be avoided, but rather embraced?

In searching for the answers to life's questions, here are thoughts you may want to consider.

First, God loves you. You may not know that, but I know that with unquestionable certainty. Believe me, God loves you more than you can possibly imagine.

Second, God knows you—inside and out, even before you were shaped and formed in your mother's womb. He knows the exact count of every hair on your head. He knows your every deed, good and bad. He knows your motives. He knows your thoughts, and He has seen every part of your life. He has witnessed every pain and every heartache. He knows your fears, your doubts, and your confusions.

Third, let me repeat it again: God loves you.

Set Yourself on Fire!

Fourth, though you may have experienced some things in your life that you may not like or even hate, God has relief for you. This relief is found in His grace—a grace that reaches down from heaven and wipes out and forgives every wrong, as if it never happened. This grace is called freedom: a freedom from guilt, shame, and anger.

Fifth, God is merciful and faithful. If we seek Him, we will find Him. This God of mercy offers forgiveness and love, and He is able to do exceedingly more for you than what you can possibly think, ask, or imagine.

The Bible says, "If we confess our sins, he is faithful and just to forgive us our sins and cleans us from all unrighteousness" (1 John 1:9).

His promises pose a new beginning and a new life!

Sixth, God desires to bless you, prosper you, and to lavish you with the abundance of life. This God of the Universe is a good God, and that is an understatement if there ever was one.

What am I saying? More important, what is God saying?

Here's the message: Life is to be embraced to the fullest. We are designed for greatness and engineered for success. All goodness that life can offer us is readily available, in insurmountable abundance. Saint Paul wrote that the "eye has not seen, nor ear heard, nor have entered into the heart of man, the things which God has prepared for those that love Him" (1 Corinthians 2:9).

The Psalmist David declared that those who delight in the law of God shall prosper. And yes, universal laws govern this world that cannot be avoided, just as there is the law of gravity and other similar laws. David went on to say that if you delight in this law, you will be like a tree planted by the rivers of water, which yields its fruit in due season, and whose leaf does not wither. Moreover, for that person, "Whatever he does, he prospers!" Now that's success, wouldn't you say? Let me repeat David's words: "Whatever he does, he prospers!" (Psalm 1:2–3).

The ancient writings of Joshua declare the very same promise. Joshua wrote, "Study this Book of Instruction continually. Meditate on it day and night so you will be sure to obey everything written in it. Only then will you prosper and succeed in all you do" (Joshua 1:8). As indicated in an earlier chapter, we become what we dwell on most. That is one of the primary keys to success.

But what if one doesn't know? Some of you may say, "I don't know. All this God stuff is a little overwhelming. Plus, I don't know who God is, if there is a God, and if He even exists. And even if He does, I don't know whether He cares or is able to relate to me."

May I suggest that if this is the case, that's a great starting point! If there is anything I know about God from my experience, it is that He is loving, kind, merciful, forgiving, understanding, and more than reasonable. God never asks anyone to do something that an individual cannot do under His provision.

The key is to be completely honest. If you don't know and are filled with questions, fears, or doubts, may I suggest that you simply talk to God.

It may sound something like this: "God, I don't know who you are. I don't know if you are even there, what you are, and if you even relate to me. But if you are, as some people say you are, and if you do exist and do care and want the best for my life, will you help me? If you are there, I want to know you, and I am asking you to fully reveal yourself to me."

God is not unreasonable. He knows the confusion of the human heart and does not turn away from those who seek Him diligently, honestly, and sincerely.

The prophet of old declared the words of God, saying, "'Come now, let us reason together,' says the LORD" (Isaiah 1:18).

Set Yourself on Fire!

I believe wholeheartedly that God will meet you right where you are. The Psalmist David declares that "the sacrifices of God are a broken spirit; a broken and contrite heart, O God, you will not despise" (Psalm 51:17).

In spite of all that others may say, I can stand here fully confident in declaring that the God of this Universe is, first and foremost, a loving God. Second, He is a reasonable, merciful, and gracious God. Third, He is a God who desires and seeks that you live life to its utmost—a life that is filled with joy, love, peace, wisdom, and goodness, and a life in which you will ultimately prosper in all that you do.

Some skeptics may respond, "I don't believe that, not for a moment!" May I suggest that those who do not believe will never have a chance to receive.

There is an age-old saying, "I'll believe it when I see it!" In reality, as Wayne Dyer writes, "You'll only see it when you believe it!"

Scripture states that according to the measure of your faith it will be rendered unto you (Matthew 9:29). Blessed, happy, are those who believe! Rarely will you see a happy skeptic. And even if having faith is a challenge, remember that God is a reasonable God. Jesus said, "If you have faith, even faith the size of a mustard seed, you can move mountains!" (Matthew 17:20).

One man came to Jesus seeking a miracle. He desired so greatly to believe, and yet it was mixed with some doubt. His heart was honest and truthful; with a heartfelt expression he blurted out, "I believe, help my unbelief!" (Mark 9:24).

Whatever faith you have, exercise that faith in the measure that it has been given to you, even if it is but one small step of faith and courage. Do this, and continue in this, and your life will eventually be transformed; ultimately you will experience the essence of what it means to be on fire! True living and true success come from seeds that are born in the fertile ground of honesty, faith, humility, and courage.

So as we come toward the end of this book, what is really being said? In short, what I've written here can be summarized into these twelve key principles:

1. Dream big. Don't settle for anything less than what completely exhilarates you. Life is too short to do anything other than to live in a manner that is consistent and in harmony with your God-given gifts.

2. Take your dreams and translate them into practical, workable ideas and plans that we call goals.

3. Cultivate the virtue of faith in what you are pursuing. Remember, "If you believe you can, you can! If you don't believe you can, you can't."

4 Just do it! There is no substitute for action.

5. Pursue your dreams with passion and enthusiasm.

6. Embrace each set of adversities as a gift. Learn to see the equal seed of opportunity in every difficulty.

7. Feed your mind continually with empowering and life-enhancing thoughts. Whatever you think about most, you become!

8. Success is a team sport. There is no such thing as a self-made man or woman. Find yourself a group of individuals who complement what you do, and who share your same vision, beliefs, and values. In doing so, you will discover the enormous power that comes with working as a team.

9. Invest in others. Realize that the most important ability and skill are found in the skill of interacting harmoniously and effectively with others.

10. In all things, joyfully deliver more than what is expected from you. This principle alone produces dividends that separate you from the crowd and put you clearly at the top of your profession.

11. Never, never, never, never give up!

12. "Commit your way unto God and He will direct your path." Seek Him first in all that you do. Pursue what is true, right, loving, and noble, and all these things will be added unto you.

Let's face it, we are all mortal beings, here only for a short period of time—a blink of an eye in the light of eternity. The author of the book of James put it in the proper perspective when he wrote that we "are just a vapor that appears for a little while and then vanishes away."

Take the risks, and seize the moment of life. Live as if it were your last day on earth, because one day it will be. Life is an unspeakable privilege, a wonderful and most blessed gift entrusted to us by our maker. Make the best use of it.

In closing, may I encourage you to be a grateful and a diligent steward of this immense privilege called living.

Love, laugh, live, and learn! And in doing so, you will have set yourself on fire!

CONCLUSION

I would rather be ashes than dust! I would rather that my spark should burn out in a brilliant blaze than it should be stifled by dry-rot. I would rather be a superb meteor, every atom of me in magnificent glow, than a sleepy and permanent planet. The function of man is to live, not to exist. I shall not waste my days trying to prolong them. I shall use my time.

   —Jack London

ABOUT THE AUTHOR

Phil Taylor is a multiple award winning speaker, trainer and internationally recognized authority on communications, sales, team performance, entrepreneurship and goal achievement.

Phil Taylor is founder of GoalAchievers International Inc., a global organization devoted to empowering individuals and organizations, through the harmonic and cooperative effort of others, to achieve extraordinary results in all areas of one's personal and business life.

Having been a top sales performer, entrepreneur, founder and owner of numerous businesses over a period of two decades, Phil knows and understands first hand the various challenges and adversities that confront individuals as they pursue excellence in their given profession.

Through his vast experience and specialized knowledge, Phil imparts his extensive insights through his colorful speeches, interactive programs, seminars and workshops, thus empowering individuals and organizations how to plan, design and achieve optimal results.

Phil lives in Toronto, Canada.

About GoalAchievers International

GoalAchievers International is a performance-driven organization that enables and empowers organizations and individuals to turn their vision into goals, and thus turn their goals into reality! It consists of a synergy of highly committed groups of individuals who meet regularly in the spirit of cooperation, harmony, trust, and definiteness of purpose to share with one another their goals in the quest to empower one another toward achievement.

Keynote Speeches

Set Yourself on Fire!...How to Ignite Your Dreams and Live the Life You Love!

It's All in How You See it!...Seeing the Equivalent Seed of Opportunity in Every Adversity!

I Believe in You!...Empowering Yourself and Others through Faith!

Slaying The Dragon!...How to Overcome Your Fears and Live Your Life with Confidence!

Go Team Go!...Turning the Ordinary into the Extraordinary through Teamwork!

The Power of Forgiveness!...Finding True Healing and Freedom through Forgiveness

Workshops and Seminars

Goal Setting and Achievement
Entrepreneurship
Leadership
Sales
Networking
Team Building
Interpersonal Communications
Public Speaking

Customized Keynotes, Workshops, and Seminars for Your Organization

Personal Coaching and Consulting Services

Goal Setting and Achievement
Small Business Development
Sales and Marketing
Public Speaking

**For More Information on Our Programs,
Please Feel Free to Call or Email**

Phone: (647) 380-8757
Email: phil@goalachievers.org

Phil Taylor as a young boy having "Set Himself on Fire!"
(Matthew 18:3)